The Black Man's Guide to Building a Global Economic Empire

Statement of Purpose: To create Black Millionaires

By

Cliff Bussey

authorHOUSE™

1663 LIBERTY DRIVE, SUITE 200
BLOOMINGTON, INDIANA 47403
(800) 839-8640
WWW.AUTHORHOUSE.COM

First published by AuthorHouse 02/24/05

ISBN: 1-4208-2338-8 (sc)

Printed in the United States of America
Bloomington, Indiana

This book is printed on acid-free paper.

Dedicated to my beloved

Mother Arlena and Father Clifton

To my Life Mother Mattie and Life Father Monroe

And to all my ancestors

Prologue

==

This is a book that should not have to be written. When I was a boy in South Carolina Black people were superior to Black people today. We didn't have our rights but what we did have was our pride and self-respect. Today we have lost both. The Black race is in a vertical decline. We have become the victims of a bought and paid for establishment, and racist businesses and non-Black tribes. Our "leaders" are not permitted to care. They lack enough love of the people to risk their income or status for the Black race.

I've personally seen the progress America has made in extending full rights to all its citizens. The country while not perfect is a far better place than it was. The progress exposed a flaw in the Black community, virulent anti-Africanism. Publicly the Black community complains about racism and that criticism is justified. They ignore the racism in the Black community that has become the major cause of our decline.

Anti-Africanism cannot be detected by looking at a Black person so it can easily be disguised, but its effects are deadly. The fact is most of the Blacks in jail or standing on street corners are dark skinned. Our "leaders" will say this is the result of racism and they're right. What they fail to mention is that it's the result of Black on Black racism. One of the worst sins in the Black community is to be born dark skinned. As a young lady once said to me, "you're a nice guy but you look so African". I didn't know any better, I thought our ancestors came from Africa. It is true that white people instituted this thinking as part of their system of control. That does not excuse Black people for continuing this terrible practice.

Almost every Black family in America has people of all shades, from black as the night to damn near white. When I was a boy I used to baby-sit my cousin. His father looked like a white man and his wife, my aunt, was light skinned resulting in him looking white. His father could easily "pass" for white but he was proud to be Black. Some Black people are ashamed of their heritage and by their actions they make it obvious.

I once had a booth at Black Expo in New York City. We were attempting to enter the computer industry. My staff was sharp, attractive and sophisticated. An elderly Black couple was impressed with our display and asked to see the headman. When the husband saw that I was dark skinned he flew into a rage and had to be physically restrained by his wife.

He constantly yelled at me "who you fronting for". I believe he would have actually fought me if not for his wife. This man was over 70 years old but his mind like those of many Blacks today was still on the plantation.

This book is not intended to change the mindset of these unchained slaves. They are a minority in the Black community. This book is intended to rally and focus the efforts of those of us who are not ashamed of our heritage. This book is about the future.

Table of Contents

Invictus

Out of the night that covers me
Black as the Pit from pole to pole
I thank whatever gods maybe
For my unconquerable soul

In the fell clutch of circumstance
I have not winced nor cried out loud
Under the bludgeonings of chance
My head is bloody but unbowed

Beyond this place of wrath and tears
Looms but the horror of the shade
And yet the menace of the years
Finds and shall find me unafraid

It matters not how strait the gate
How charged with punishment the scroll
I am the Master of my fate
I am the Captain of my soul

William Earnest Henley

Overview

Let me start out by saying that I'm a victim of the white man's educational system. I actually believe in most aspects of Western ideology. I admire Sir Isaac Newton (science), Adam Smith (economics), Henry Ford, Thomas Edison, Dr. Drew (medicine), Dr. Martin Luther King (human rights), etc. I don't admire them because they're white or Black I admire them for what they did to help mankind. We have to get over this racial thing. White people are doing a better job of it than we are. We need to take advantage of our position in the world. We are extremely powerful. Our problem is that we're not using our power. The civil rights war has been fought and we won. It's time to use American technology to develop Black America, Africa, the Caribbean, Brazil, etc. We'll finance it. We can all be rich.

I remember when Roots was on television. A white friend of mine was very concerned about the way white people were portrayed. She asked me "where are the good white people" in Roots. I looked under my desk and said "I can't find any". I thought I was clever but later realized that this was my friend and my response was inappropriate. Sometime you have to consider the other person's position. It makes you stronger.

There is a choice facing man in the near future. The choice is going to be whether powerful nations have the right to take the land of weaker nations. This crisis will be the result of certain limitations concerning Earth's resources. If everybody on Earth consumed resources at the rate that Americans do we'd need 3 1/2 Earths. We have to use the Earth's resources more efficiently. America is the best hope for the people of the world if it can correct is flaws. I'm convinced that Black people would be much better of just being Americans. We need to join the American economy as full players.

50,000 years ago the ancestors of all people living today lived in Africa according to almost all reputable scientists including Spencer Wells. Mr. Wells is the author of "Journey of Man, A Genetic Odyssey". Mr. Wells' DNA analysis indicates that the oldest people living today are the San people of Namibia. There are dozens of theories about how man evolved but there's no doubt where he came from. Man is an African animal. Everybody says so. I learned this when I took a course in anthropology at the Fashion Institute of Technology in New York City. I've often read and seen the same thing over a hundred times on TV, on the Internet and in print.

Germans, Chinese, Mexicans, Russians, Iranians, etc. are all children of Africa. Scientifically, we are the original men. That's what makes the current situation in the African American community so ironic. These people that are referred to as white, Asian, Latino, etc. are actually our descendants. We're setting a terrible example.

Today Africa is known for poverty, disease and political chaos.

African Americans are known for crime and sports and entertainment figures that are increasingly pride-less.

We must assume to our proper place.

The purpose of this book is to be the first step in building an African American global economic empire. This book presents what I believe is a workable strategy that will solve a basic problem: Black economic weakness.

African American income was $552,000,000,000.00 in the year 2000 according to the United States Census Bureau. All this spending has little or no positive effect on the Black community. Money goes out and never comes back. This is not natural in economics. I believe the most effective way to end the chronic problem of Black poverty is to provide an easy, honest and realistic way for Blacks to invest. They must see results, not just listen to promises. A plan of action is needed now! The situation is dire and will only worsen if we continue with our very destructive behavior and unrealistic beliefs.

The Black male must step up. Some of our females will assist us, but most won't until they see results. We need to embark on a new strategy. We need a strategy based on our strengths and not our weaknesses. We need to have a plan that depends on us, not the good graces of others.

I am confident this book will be perceived by Black people who have real pride as an effort to solve some of our major problems. Those who are just talking Black will resent it just as they resent anybody with real pride. I am prepared to put the strategy present in this book up against anybody's strategy. The strategy in this book depends on Black people.

If a very small percentage of the Black community joins us, success is assured. The situation is beyond serious. I intend to use some of the royalties from the sale of this book to form an investment firm. For purposes of presentation I will call the investment firm "The Company".

The Company is designed specifically to create a Black economic empire. I've decided not to make to make this book long or complex. This is a plan for the people. It must be able to be understood by the people, even those hanging out on the street corner.

You can march, protest, and do flip-flops but nothing is going to provide jobs or a future for Black people except investment by Black people. It's silly to believe that politics will result in success. You can whine and moan all you want but unless we get our act together, we will become extinct.

At least once every week we hear that the Black male is becoming extinct. This is not just talk. This is a real possibility. I've read where people are already complaining that Africans are not using the resources of the continent properly. In one case I read about a Chinese man who was really upset. Black people have been lulled into a false sense of security. We are so psychologically dependent on white people that when you mention trying to do something for ourselves you might as well be speaking Greek.

Even our educated people are psychologically dependent. They are in many respects more brainwashed than people hanging out on a street corner. Numerous times I've seen educated Blacks act as if they're afraid that someone will notice they're Black if they speak to another Black in the business district. They have a deep hostility towards Blackness.

They're victims. Their bodies are free but sadly, for many their minds are still on the plantation.

Many times you will see Black financial experts on cable TV business shows giving advice to the public. I've often wondered why they never come up with a plan for the Black community. Think about it.

In order to present the plan to the Black community I decided to put the plan in book form.

The plan will be explained in the remaining pages of this book.

What is Power?

Power is having over 30 Hispanic television programs on cable in the Bronx in New York City in 2004 at the same time. Hispanics have power. The Powers That Be know they must respect Hispanics. They know that if they don't respect Hispanics it will cost them money, big time money. Jews have 1 United States Senator per 1,200,00 American Jews. If Blacks has US Senators at the same rate there'd be 30 Black United States Senators. Jews, Hispanics and other groups get respect because they respect themselves. They have good people and bad people just as we do, but the good people dominate in other communities. In reality Blacks have no power. Our masters have discovered a chink in our armor and they're exploiting it. They know that we lack unity and self esteem. Black entertainers, athletes and public officials have money and/or status but they have very little power.

In my opinion the most powerful athletes are retired. George Foreman and Magic Johnson have power. Many of today's Black athletes have big time salaries but they don't have real power. They cannot make a final decision on their own or in reality be a decisive player in basic business decisions. Magic Johnson and Big George can. So can Oprah. Louis Farrakhan had enough power to get a million men together in peace. This was supposed to be impossible. What The Million Man March proved was that there is a deep frustration among proud Black males about how we're being treated and what's going on in the community. I didn't go and but I took the day off. Some of my friends went including some people I didn't think were interested in Black issues. I've heard that there were agent provocateurs on the trains coming from Washington to New York after the Million Man March. People I know told me that there were some white guys on the train calling people nigger and making other racist remarks. Evidently the plan was to incite violence between these agents and Black males heading back to New York City. The proof is that when the train arrived in New York the press was waiting and acted as they expected something to be happening. The Brothers were on to it from the beginning. Why would a group of white guys start calling people nigger in a train full of Black men? Since they weren't on a suicide mission I must assume that they were acting under orders. All I can say is that the way my friends tell it the media was waiting expectantly.

Speaking of the racist media, I was amazed at the brouhaha over LeBron James Hummer and contract. What was he supposed to do? Sportswriters were complaining that he should have gone to college. Since he wasn't Donald Trump's son he had to go for the money. Black people must remember that sportswriters are different now. When Babe Ruth was playing he did outrageous things but it was considered manly. The Babe wasn't Black either but he was called nigger quite a lot. If a Black athlete stumps his toe it's going to be on the evening news. Sportswriters are extremely jealous of these young Black males earning all this money. They say "go to college" and I agree but you would have to be stupid to turn down millions of dollars to go to college. You can always go later. Take the money and run.

Back to power

There was one "Black" network and it treated us like nothing. Now there are none. Blacks in the entertainment industry are much weaker than Black athletes. They have almost no influence at all. Those with pride must grin and bear it as they try to make a living in the most racist industry in America, the media. The others are just people who would sell their souls for their 15 seconds of fame. Pride demands that we must finance our own media. The Company has a plan.

Geraldo Rivera in my opinion is the most anti-Black person on TV. What he does to Black people is like someone urinating in your face and telling you it's raining. Also I heard that Whoopi Goldberg said that "nigger" is just a word. I believe she converted to Judaism and I dare her to say publicly that "kike" is just a word. With today's technology we don't have to deal with racists or Blacks with no pride. When we have 5 Black television stations in New York I'll be satisfied, a little. If we had 5 stations we could put on programs that show us in a normal light. Now we're either going to jail, in some scandal involving public funds, an ignorant Black athlete cursing on prime time TV, or some other negative image. We have to aspire to power.

Knowledge

This is the weakest part of our armor. Knowledge, like character, has no status in Black America. People who could possibly find a cure for cancer or design a skyscraper are discouraged in our community from exhibiting their talent. It's cool to be a fool. If you're in the know, be a ho. Everyone who is knowledgeable is better off than they would be without knowledge. The world doesn't owe anybody anything as my uncle Monroe used to say. Black people can go around playing the gangsta, bitch and ho if they want to but in the end we will disappear if we don't change. There are about 2,000,000 East Indians in America. 400,000 of them are millionaires. If you know some of them it's obvious why. They are very educated. They have degrees in hard subjects like engineering, computers, physics, math, chemistry, finance, etc. India mass produces highly educated people. India has a bright future.

A lot of Black people gravitate to easy courses that require a lot less work to obtain a degree. This is a mistake. Young Black people are judged by their ability to fight, their car, ability to act a fool or the number of sexual conquests. Girls are in this competition also and are using more profane language than boys in public. If you want to acquire knowledge you're accused of acting "white" according to the new ideology. In fact anything positive is white. Shakespeare is not a great writer because he is white. He's a great writer because he really is a great writer. Sometimes a cigar is just a cigar. I was introduced to Shakespeare in junior high school and it has made me a better person. I'll even watch a Shakespeare play if I see it on the TV schedule. He had to be a good man, after all he said to kill all the lawyers. Have you ever wondered why the moon is so bright on nights when there is a full moon? It turns out that the moon's surface is 30 to 60% glass.

2 of the most innocent meek looking people you've ever seen are Capt. Kangaroo and Mr. Rogers. These were two of the most dangerous people you could encounter if you were in a battle against them. Capt. Kangaroo fought on Iwo Jima in World War 2. Iwo Jima was a slaughterhouse. Mr. Rogers personally killed over 20 people when he was a Special Forces member. The reason he always wore sweaters was to cover up all the tattoos on his arms. I like knowing things as you can probably surmise.

I attended Fordham University at the Lincoln Center campus in New York City. I was studying for my double degree in Economics & Business when a friend suggested that we go see a Shakespeare play in the auditorium. A friend of ours was in the play and she twisted my arm and we went to see it. She didn't have to twist too hard because believe me, she was gorgeous. It was a production of Othello and one of our friends had the leading role. Our friend was Denzel Washington. Knowledge of Shakespeare certainly didn't hurt him.

A person should be willing to learn from others regardless of the source. Why do you think wealthy people from around the world send their children here to go to college?

We have to take advantage of our being here, not whine about it. The slaves are dead and can't be freed, but we can be free if we have the will to be. Knowledge increases your self-confidence. People will respect you if you're knowledgeable. For instance did you know that the word algebra is actually a form of an Arab mathematician's name?

If you know some history, science, music, current events, sports, etc. you can always hold your own in a conversation. In our community all knowledge is "white" and as a result we reject anything from them except Cadillac's, jewelry, airplanes, cell phones, etc. We desire the products of knowledge but reject knowledge itself.

In Roman times thumbs up meant death, not life. Thumbs down meant let him live. In every movie you see now thumbs down means death, this is the exact opposite of the truth. We must move to a knowledge-based philosophy.

The reason I believe knowledge is not encouraged is that in order to convey knowledge to the masses you have to deal with the masses. In addition many parents have psychologically rejected their offspring. After a Diana Ross concert in Central Park the New York Times ran an editorial about the violet behavior of some of the concertgoers. I was there and it was terrible. The Times editorial stated that Blacks lacked self-esteem and that even their parents rejected these youths. I was incensed at the time but I have to admit it's true. Black on Black rejection is a normal occurrence in our community. If we are to survive this is an issue that must dealt with. Sir Isaac Newton's 3rd Law of Motion states that "for every action there is an equal and opposite reaction". Black on Black discrimination results in the rejected rejecting the values and beliefs of the discriminators. This is the basis of the hip-hop culture. The Black elite looked down on the Black masses and they developed their culture that distained everything that the Black ruling class aspired to.

I Once Had My Shoes Shined

I had a job at the airport where I was managing 8 businesses at once, restaurants, bars, and a club. There was a white man who used to shine shoes there. I knew this man and we joked around every day before my shift started. Then one day it happened. I came to work early. I had some extra time so I decided to get a shoeshine from my friend. I'm sitting in the chair joking with him but I then noticed that he looked uncomfortable. Then I saw some of my bosses walk by and they were not smiling. What I didn't realize then but realized later was that I committed a great sin.

I had humiliated a white man by having him shine my shoes. I thought he was a shoeshine man, I didn't know any better. If he were Black he wouldn't have been offended. The point I'm trying to make is that a lot of white people are not comfortable with Black progress. They're very insecure. You can't tell by looking at them which ones are like this. An insecure non-Black person will not work with us and that's great! We don't need them anyway. There are plenty of confident people to assist us in our quest.

As to why our "leadership" won't tackle problems like this. Ask them.

What I think is on the next page

It Is and It Is Not

It's very puzzling what the Black establishment's goal is in terms of our people's future

It is not to build pride in our people

It is not to build up a Black economic base

It is not to establish strategic relationships with other Americans

It is not to trade with Africa

It is not to build manufacturing facilities in Black areas

It is not to uphold family unity

It is not to work with American business

It is not to really educate our people

It is not to look to the future

It is however, planned failure

The Current Problem

There is no way Black people are going to progress without direct investment in us by us. I've known and I'm sure many of you have known Black people with great ideas but their ideas simply die. Why shouldn't Black people have a chance to fulfill their dreams like everyone else? Their dreams go nowhere because there's no way to finance them. Others are not going to finance our dreams for us. It's an insult for anyone to encourage you to believe otherwise. Forget the government.

Other people will assist us if there's something in it for them. That something is money. Despite what Black "leaders" are telling you white people aren't holding us back. Our own establishment is holding us back because deep in their souls they associate blackness with inferiority. Just look at who's on the street corner. Almost all of them are dark skinned. This is not an accident. Sure white people divided us by skin color, gender, age, etc. but do we have to perpetuate this stupid behavior? Those who exploit us know that we discriminate against each other and depend on that to keep us in economic bondage.

It has gotten so bad that internationally the word "black" has become a synonym for loser, low class, foreigner, etc. In Japan, non-Japanese Asians are called black. In Russia people from the southern part of the country who have black hair and that are discriminated against are called black. In Israel Jews whose ancestors are not from Europe and who are discriminated against are called black. Black is becoming a global term for the incapable, the weak, and the dumb.

Black people have to separate social preferences from economic needs. I'm dark skinned but I'd prefer to give my money to a Black person of any shade then to these evil racist merchants in our community now. Who you want to party with has nothing to do with making money. If we can't overcome our social brainwashing and get on with making money, we are finished. Other people will not do this for us.

Would you believe that Germany, the nation that gave us Nazism is currently building submarines for the ANC led government of South Africa right now. Things change. Daimler-Chrysler forced German autoworkers to give $600 million in concessions in order to keep their jobs. Daimler-Chrysler threatened to send 6,000 jobs to South Africa if they did not submit. The point I'm trying to make is that in today's world economics trumps almost everything.

The problem with solving these problems is that you can't tell anything about a person by looking at them. Not all the merchants in our community are anti-Black, but most are. Whether they like Blacks or not will become irrelevant. The Company will open Black owned store en masse.

We cannot fail if 3 to 5 percent of us work together. Many times people will say that everybody will not cooperate. When it comes to humans the words "everybody" and "all" are ridiculous. Most white people are not racists and most Blacks are not criminals. Most people are followers so all you need is a core of people who walk the walk and not just talk the talk. 3 to 5 percent of the Black people in America are more than enough.

The biggest problem we have is discrimination by skin color in the Black community. 400 years of brainwashing is not going to disappear overnight. We must be honest about this because it must be overcome. Pretending that white people are our major obstacle won't get it done. Our people must learn to divide social from economic issues.

It's not important if somebody doesn't like somebody as long as we're making money. You can love yourself. If you're doing the right thing others are going to like you too.

The Company will not take skin color into account when making decisions. Anyone who has ever been in the military knows that Black people of all shades are successful in that environment. Why this doesn't happen in the civilian economy? After all, the military is run by white Christian males isn't it? Blacks can succeed in the military because it a merit based organization.

It doesn't happen in civilian life mainly because the Black establishment discriminates against dark skinned Blacks so heavily. Sure white racism plays a role, but it's a minor one now. Many dark skinned Blacks are shunned from the time most of them are born. Some parents and grandparents treat children differently based on skin color. One thing I can saw about my family is that I never felt or saw that. The Company cannot stop this but it can make people aware of what their doing and the consequences thereof.

The Company will open up new opportunities for everybody. If a white investor is a carpenter and a Black carpenter is not then the white carpenter will get the contract. If the white carpenter knows that The Company plans to uplift the Black community and still wants to invest he will be treated like any other investor.

The current system is useless to us. We don't have the experience nor do we have the infrastructure to build an economic empire. However we can build the institutions needed if we apply our will power.

I'm also the president of a startup company named Bussey Energia. Bussey Energia came up with a miraculous design for a machine that could solve many problems faced by man in the fields of energy, information and health. One of the best universities in the world has agreed to build the prototypes for us. We have a great staff made up of some of the best minds available. People in the solar energy business said we would attain great wealth. Yet we could not obtain financing or even an offer.

Most of Bussey Energia's stockholders are Black-working people, women and men. There are also whites, Hispanics and Asians in Bussey Energia. I included information on our company's invention in this book in order to show how difficult it is for Black people to obtain financing. I guess it didn't help that I named 2 models Kilimanjaro and Zulu. If we couldn't get financing with this then you know others can forget it. The following pages include the Executive Summary of Bussey Energia's Business Plan. The Summary will give you an idea of what we are trying to build. There are also graphic designs of the machine from the Business Plan. I hope you will find it interesting.

1.0 Executive Summary

Bussey Energia is seeking investment in order to initiate Bussey Energia's strategic plan. Bussey Energia's goal is to be #1 in the emerging solar and fuel cell energy delivery and power utilization market. The investment will be used to build production quality prototypes of the Kilimanjaro and Starship energy and utilization systems, and invest in an advanced artificial intelligence company.

Bussey Energia has invented a new type of product, the Lifestyle Enhancement Machine (LEM). We believe the consumer will easily see the superiority of our designs and concept. Consumers will easily realize that our products are much more than just solar energy delivery systems. Our machines will improve the very lives of their owners by providing energy, information and entertainment. Bussey Energia has contracted The University of Dayton's Research Institute to build the prototypes.

The Research Institute's Kettering Lab is one of the premiere prototype facilities in the United States. The Lab is particularly adept at system engineering, which integrates different engineering disciplines (i.e. structural, instrumentation & controls, hydraulics & pneumatics, energy conversion, etc.) in response to overall product performance requirements. The Kettering Lab is a registered ISO 9001, which means they develop and follow recognized design practices and fabrication processes including developing design requirements, holding design reviews, and validating product performance before releasing the product to the customer. The Kettering Lab's in-house technical resources have developed an extensive list of approved vendors for supplying materials, transducers, and software and fabrication services. NASA, GE, the US Air Force are just a few of the Labs former customers.

Bussey Energia has also contracted Home Automated Living, Inc. (HAL) to develop an advanced artificial intelligence system to control the LEM and act as the interface between the LEM owner and the machine. Bussey Energia has also negotiated an agreement to take an equity position in Home Automated Living after an Initial Public Offering (IPO). The LEM will speak and translate English, French, Spanish, Italian, German, Mandarin Chinese, Hindi and Zulu. HAL will be able to control the LEM and home appliances in the home from anywhere in the world at the owner's request. The HAL system *(HAL Maximus)* will also be a stand-alone product that will be marketed as the most advanced home artificial intelligence system.

Bussey Energia believes that solar energy, wind, fuel cell and hydrogen power will become the main sources of power on Earth. Our designs, which are stand alone systems, can deliver power from all these sources while covering much less of the Earth surface than other energy delivery systems.

Bussey Energia's Lifestyle Enhancement Machines (LEMs) are Earth friendly machines designed to improve the lifestyle of their owners. Bussey Energia believes that the LEM concept will become generally accepted. The LEM will enhance the consumers' lifestyle whether they're rich or poor. LEMs are vertical solar energy machines that require relatively little Earth surface.

LEMs will provide electricity courtesy of the Sun, electricity from wind power, and electricity from fuel cells, provide fuel from hydrogen, provide global communications, speech recognition and catch and clean water. It can provide hot water, entertainment, education, and all the while being a beautiful work of art. In the developing world, a single LEM capable of powering the average American home will be able to provide power for several homes or be the basis of a school. LEMs will also provide power for irrigation, water purification, and light at night, cooking, communications, and education and information via the Internet. Powerful wind turbines will be options on LEMs. In windy areas or during the night or day, LEMs with wind turbines will still be working to supply the consumer's needs.

Bussey Energia believes everyone on Earth is a potential customer. In order to live a decent life on planet Earth you need electricity and clean water. Bussey Energia believes that its LEM business will rival an automobile company in size. LEMs will be upgradeable. The solar arrays and other components can be replaced with more efficient parts as technology advances.

The Bussey Energia's LEMs will be able to be scaled up or down to power homes, microwave stations or assembled in a configuration of giant LEMs enough power to light a small city. Fresh water is increasingly becoming a global issue that in some cases can lead to war. LEMs can avert these scenarios. Modern desalination techniques have reduced the cost of taking the salt out of seawater to $2 per 1,000 gallons. Giant LEMs can be configured with filtering equipment and put along the coast lines and easily solve the global fresh water problem. It will also be practical to pump the water and hydrogen produced from water hundreds of miles inland. This will make large areas of the Earth practical to live on. LEM powered pumping stations could be positioned along the pipeline to power the pumps and provide hydrogen.

The LEMs are divided into several modules, each contributes to the lifestyle enhancement of the owner in its own way:

1. The Communications System and Artificial Intelligence System: The LEMs will contain a wireless Internet connection, an advanced HAL artificial intelligence system (HAL Maximus) that eventually be able to teach any subject, to anyone, in any language, anywhere.

2. The Energy Delivery System: The internal area of the Turret consists of solar panels. This will induce manufacturers to make panels this will fit into Bussey Energia's designs. The big advantage of the LEMs Energy Delivery System over other solar systems is that LEMs expose more solar panels at 90 degrees for a longer period of time than other designs. In other words, a 100 solar watt panel on a LEM will deliver 20% more energy than a 100-watt panel on a fixed design. A regenerative fuel cell system will be a basic component of the Energy Delivery System (see the University of Dayton's Research Institute contract). The contract is not included in this book for obvious reasons.

3. The Artists' Canvas: The LEM will be work of art in itself. The machines will be manufactured in colors such as gold, silver, bronze, etc. The LEM can be customized on the

outside at the request of the customer. We envision that artists will take to this just as they take to detailing automobiles. Bussey Energia will offer several art options. This will be a major enticement to customers in the industrialized nations .

4. The Sun Location System: The Sun Location System consists of a light sensor and a global positioning system. The light sensor will find the position of the Sun, and the LEM, which can turn 300 degrees, will adjust the position of the solar panels for maximum energy production.

5. The Clean Water System: The Clean Water System is made up of the Rain/Snow Catcher, filters, and water tanks in the LEM. If it snows the Catcher will simply heat itself and melt the snow or ice.

6- The Modular Unit: The Modular Unit is for customization by the LEMs' owner. The water tanks are in the Modular Unit. The consumer can order a regenerative fuel cell system, electrical outlets, hydrogen production equipment or other special machines. Since LEMs have 4 sides it would be possible for a family in their backyard to watch 2 different TV's, Bar-B-Q, play music and surf the Internet all at the same time. On a farm the special machines could be irrigation pumps. It would be economical for a farmer to put a LEM in his field. The modular unit could contain giant water tanks and pumping equipment only.

In the developing world where electricity is unreliable or non-existent, a LEM could power several homes and provide a gateway to the world because of the wireless Internet connection. The special machine could be a water purification system placed in the Modular Unit. The threat of dirty water will become one of the great challenges facing man. The LEM's Modular Unit is designed to encourage companies to manufacture components that will be installed in it. The Modular unit will also contain HAL Maximus who will run the LEM. Home appliance control software, voice recognition software and software that will allow technicians to analyze problems over the Internet will be in the Modular Unit computer.

Solar technology is advancing rapidly. According to *Time* magazine the cost per watt has declined 71% in the last decade. All LEM components will be designed to be replaced. A LEM that will supply 80% of the home's energy needs today will supply 120% in the future as solar technology advances. A LEM owner need only trade-in his old solar panels for new ones. The LEM itself will be part of the family. The LEM owner has to simply insert the more efficient solar panels, just as computers are upgraded now. Home owners will be able to sell the excess energy back to the power grid. While the homeowner is on vacation they can be making money selling the daily energy production of their LEM.

Eventually a standard LEM the homeowner buys today will provide excess power tomorrow. In the USA there are large tax credits and other incentives offered by local governments, states and the Federal government for installing solar energy systems. The developing world is an excellent market for LEMs. The great advantage of the LEMs is that they're kinetic when it comes to the owner's lifestyle. Other solar systems just provide power and heat water. Electric grills, TV's, stereo equipment. small ice boxes, etc. can be connected directly to a LEM. LEMs will also be works of art, the neighbors will have to have one! The

LEM will also be an interesting, environmentally correct conversation piece for it's owner to explain to the neighbors.

As far as the impact of the LEM is concerned regarding business and industry, consider the following possibilities:

Businesses: Businesses will find Bussey Energia LEMs' very appealing. A company in the suburbs could offer office hour free electric vehicle battery charges or hydrogen fuel as job benefits. LEMs would also be great for companies seeking to reduce their utility bills and can also serve as an emergency power source. Parking lot owners can charge fees for charging electric vehicles in addition to the parking fees they currently collect. Shopping centers can offers free or discounted vehicle charges as an incentive to visit. Hotels can all find this strategy very profitable.

Real Estate Developers: Real estate developers could offer Bussey Energia LEMs as part of a new home package. The LEM could become a standard for new homes.

Developing Nations: In many parts of the Earth, the 2 main problems is the lack of a source of power and clean water. Since LEMs are stand-alone systems they can solve these problems easily. Afghanistan, South America and Africa are perfect places to put LEMs. Southern California is also. With its' built in communications capacity a LEM will also open the entire world of knowledge to the most remote area. For a developing nation the cost of a single conventional power plant that has to constantly be fed expensive fuel, a LEM grid composed of giant LEMs is a better investment. In a village a LEM could provide clean water.

Clean water alone will prevent many infectious diseases. LEMs with special machines for teaching could educate an entire village. They could learn about crop rotation, prices paid for the crops they raise, mathematics, world news, etc. Bussey Energia's strategy is have final assembly plants in several countries. This will result in greater cooperation from local governments because it will be a source of quality jobs for the local population.

Electric Vehicle & Fuel Cell Vehicle Manufacturers: The biggest problem with electric and/or fuel cell vehicles is that they are not practical to use. The main problem is charging your electric vehicle or obtaining hydrogen. LEMs can spur electric/fuel cell vehicle production by providing a practical solution to this problem. When the electric/fuel cell car owner is home his car can be connected to the LEM and charged or refueled with hydrogen. In the evening the LEM can charge the car with energy saved from the daylight hours.

Military: The military needs a mobile power system that requires a minimum of support in order to supply power. Special LEMs can be made to military specifications.

Bussey Energy is confident that the time has come for our concept. The global warming and the energy crisis are only going to get worse. Clean water is increasingly mentioned in the headlines. Bussey Energia is ready!

1.1 Objectives

BUSSEY ENERGIA GOALS:

- Build and test the Kilimanjaro and Starship prototypes.

- Build a staff of trained professionals who can run Bussey Energia's operations.

- Become the major brand name in the solar energy/fuel cell fields.

- Prepare and execute an Initial Public Offering within 1.5 years.

- Complete a facility to mass-produce LEMs within 2 to 3 years.

The following pages are illustrations Of

Bussey Energia's Lifestyle Enhancement Machines

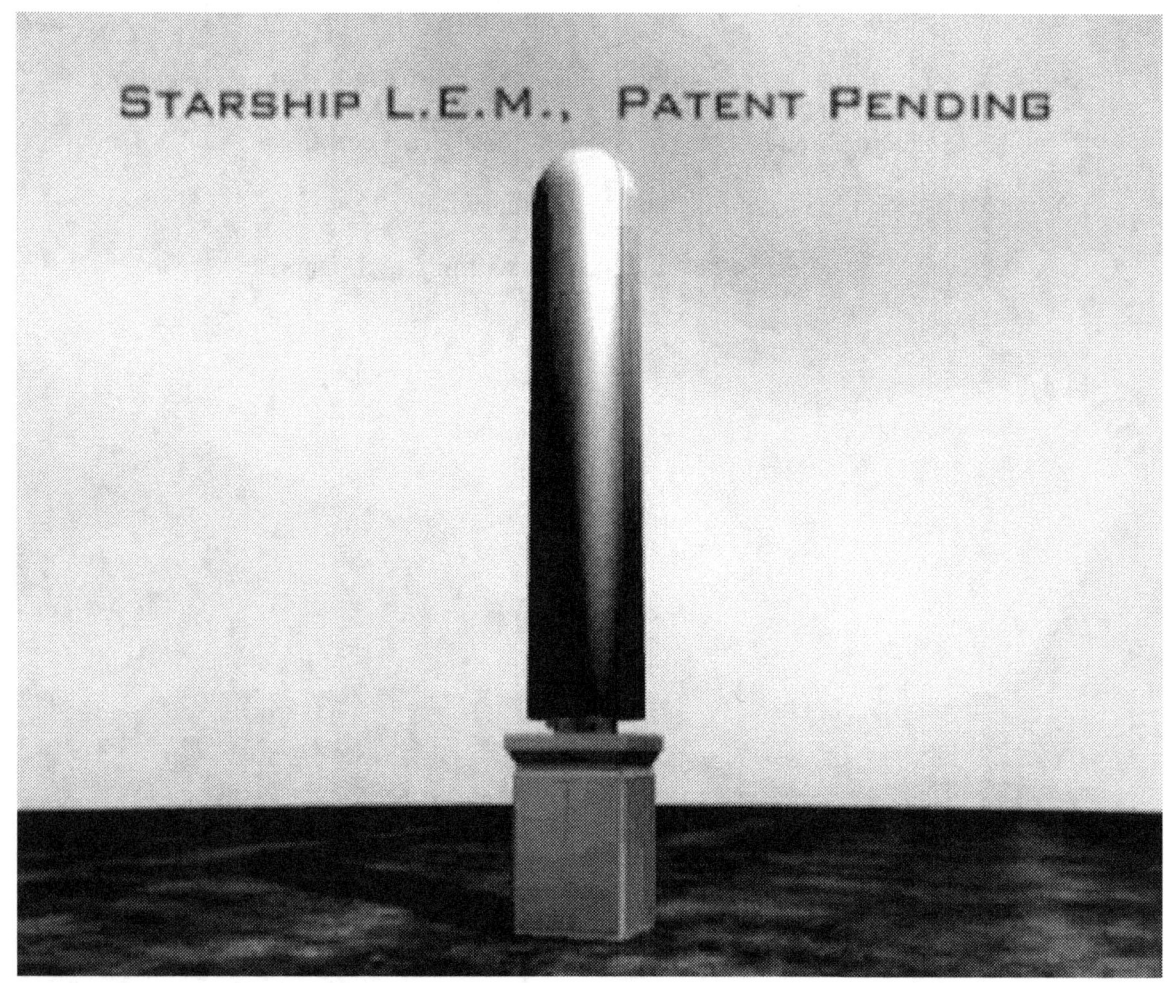

The Starship models are:

The Starship von Braun
Named after the designer of the Saturn 5 moon rocket

The Starship Gagarin
Named for Yuri Gagarin, the first man in space

1 wind turbine
The Starship Americanus

The people who made to the moon
2 wind turbines

LEM's open to expose their solar panels to the light of the Sun. When light touches the panels a flow of electrons is created. The electricity is stored in the lower part of the machine until it is needed for use. The machine has no batteries. The energy is stored in the form of hydrogen and oxygen atoms. The LEM will break up water by electrolysis of water. Later the LEM will re-combine the hydrogen and oxygen atoms to create water. This re-combining creates an electrical current that can be used at night.

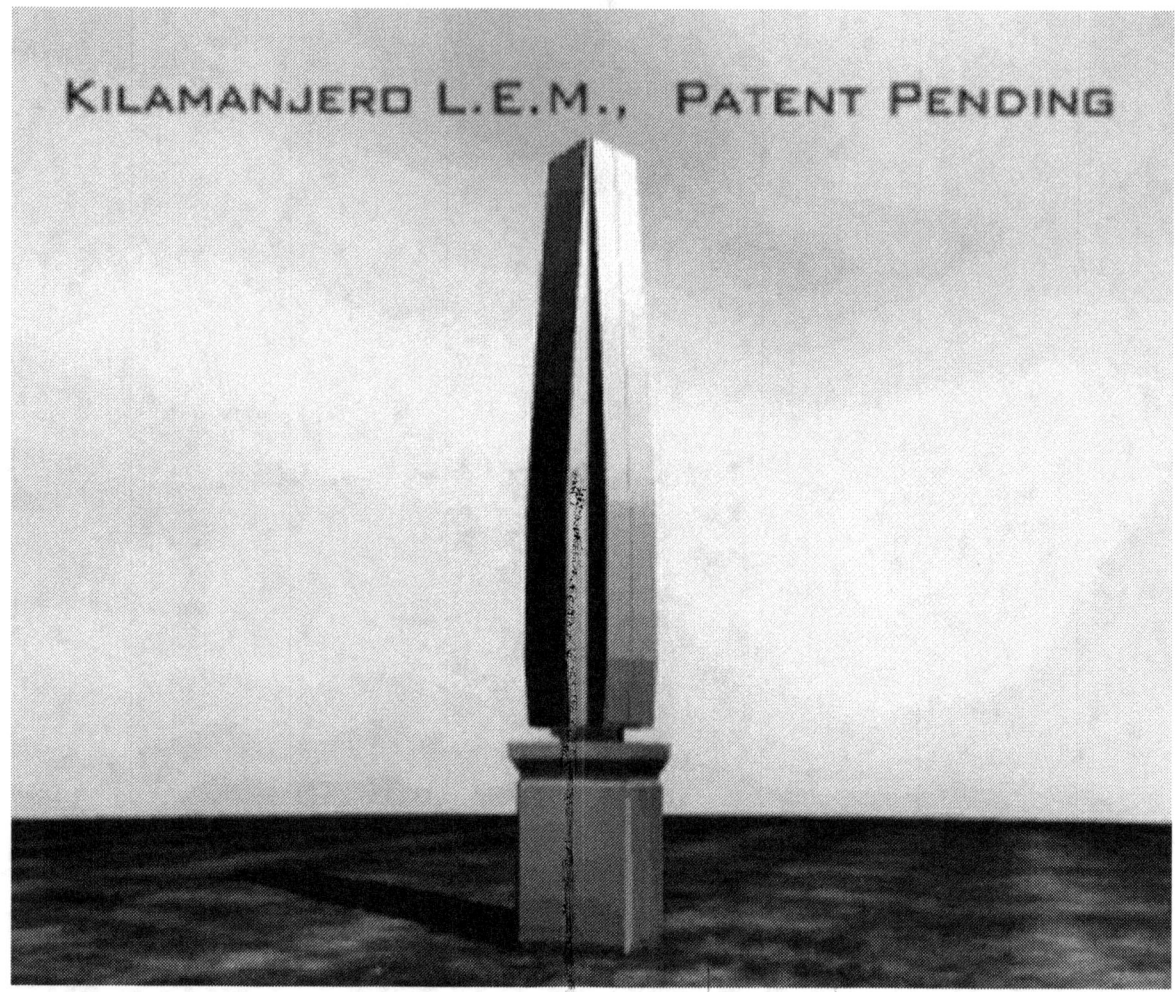

I know Kilimanjaro is misspelled. Mount Kilimanjaro is the highest mountain in Africa.

The Kilimanjaro models are:

Kilimanjaro ER
Eleanor Roosevelt
Civil rights heroine and First Lady of the United States

Kilimanjaro Winston
Winston Churchill
A great leader and thinker
1 wind turbine

Kilimanjaro Zulu
2 wind turbines

The LEM will be able to break down water into hydrogen and oxygen. The hydrogen can then be used to power automobiles.

In addition to powering 1 or even 2 homes the LEM will provide power for backyard entertaining. Any electrical appliance can be attached directly to a LEM.

The Starship Americanus with 2 wind turbines. Powerful wind turbines can be attached to LEMs to provide power on windy days or nights.

My Conclusions

One of the features of the current Black enslavement is denial of access to capital. I've known many Black people who had great, creative and ingenious ideas. They all run up against the same problem I did. We did not get a single offer. I know that business decisions are cold and hard. There's no room from for affirmative action in a serious business decision. If my machine could do what we said it could it would be a great bargain for an investor. We only needed $4,000,000. Experts on the solar energy field said it was a great concept. People in the solar energy business said I would have a monopoly and yet nobody was interested. We had one of the best research labs in the country to build the machines. The University of Dayton has over 300 scientists, engineers, etc. at its disposal. Home Automated Living is a leader in artificial intelligence. My staff includes some of the best minds available. Yet we did not get an offer.

I've always admired men like Booker T. Washington and George Washington Carver. Mr. Carver invented so many things it's mind-boggling. Synthetic rubber, plastic, mayonnaise, shoe polish, and adhesives are just a few. There are many Black inventors that should be seen as role models for Black youth. Dr. George E. Alcorn invented a method of fabricating an imaging x-ray spectrometer. Dr. Patricia Booth patented a method of removing cataract lenses making eye surgery safer and more accurate. Otis Boykin created electrical devices used in missiles and computers. Marie Brown patented a video home security system.

The story of one inventor is really different. Benjamin Banneker built the first watch built in America in 1753. His father Banna Ka, was an African slave. His mother Molly Walsh was an English indentured servant. Molly Walsh bought Banna Ka and another African. Molly Wash became Banna Ka's wife. Benjamin Banneker knew Thomas Jefferson and questioned his sincerity about liberty considering the fact that Jefferson himself was a slave owner.

Black people are not ever going to prosper under this current system. We have to ignore the current financial system. We have to reach a better compromise between profits and the public good. The Government is working against us economically. The Government does not assist our self-development. The effect of government policies is that non-Blacks are investing in our communities and denying opportunities to our people. We must adjust the way business is done in Black neighborhoods. We must form our own capital base so we don't have to go and beg others. It would be stupid to expect other people to finance real Black economic progress. As Bob Dylan said in the song Like a Rolling Stone, "when you ain't got nothing you got nothing to lose". We have nothing so therefore we have nothing to lose.

I believe in simple things like grocery stores, restaurants, clothing stores, appliance stores, etc. These are the kinds of businesses that drive communities to wealth. Forget about the current establishment. If they were going to do something they would have done it long ago. The masses must act.

Currently in the community if you run a bank, a grocery owner, a fast food place, etc., you can ignore Black interests. Why should you hire a Black person when you're going to get their money anyway? Blacks don't have alternatives. Even if the guy on the corner cheats your children you still have to go buy there again. You can go to another store but you're going to get the same treatment. You're never giving your money to another Black person. I always calculate my total bill when I go to these stores. Over a dozen times I had to "correct" the total bill and get all my change. If you notice many stores have material in front of the register so you can't see the numbers being added.

That's OK. If this is the way they want to deal, then we'll play the hand we've been dealt.

That is what this book is about

The Black Community

It has become obvious that the current strategy for dealing with the problems in the African American community is not going to work. Year after year it's the same. Every other ethnic group in America is building an economic base except Blacks. Capitalism, the natural solution is banned from discussion in our community. Our current tactics will NEVER work for the vast majority. What we need is a feasible plan that depends on actions that we take and not the decisions of others.

We are in a psychological state where we constantly discriminate against each other for the benefit of others. Black people constantly complain about white people but the truth is that white people treat us better than we treat each other. As Sir Charles Barkley said, Black people treat each other like crap. Our pride and cohesion has been completely destroyed with the willing assistance of "black leaders".

I was at a meeting in Harlem with many other Black business wannabees. The meeting was about the Harlem Empowerment Zone that was being organized. The chair of the meeting, a former Manhattan Borough President and a prominent member of the Black community in New York asked everyone in the room to introduce themselves. There were about 40 people in the room. All the Blacks including myself introduced themselves. Finally the chair got to 3 white males seated next to him and he then said "now we get to the real power". Everyone was outraged. How could he insult a room full of Black people like that? Unfortunately he was right as Harlem's development has proven. Black people have no say so even in their own community.

Let's take a very visible example of our degradation; manners. Black people used to be very respectful. Even though we were segregated and limited in what we could accomplish, we still had our pride. We were especially respectful of the elderly, women and children. Now Black people give each other absolutely no respect at all. Why not call each other nigger in public. It's all right to say nigger in records isn't it?

Now it is not only "cool" to be disrespectful but to be loud while doing it.

Dr. Cosby is right. A lot of Black parents are not parenting at all. You can buy kids the latest and the greatest material thing but if you don't instill values in your child, they will fail. Even as I write this book I see examples of how low we have fallen. In the June 19, 2004 edition of the New York Post (page 7) there are two articles about murders. In both cases the killings were senseless. In one case a young girl was killed by her "friend" over iced tea. Iced tea is worth more than a human life? Apparently so to some people. In the other case two 15-year-old boys killed a homeless man for fun by hitting him with 40 bricks. As usual the killers and the victims were Black. The more senseless the act, the more likely the perpetrators are Black. The best civil rights bill passed in a long time was the 3 strikes and you're out crime bill. Many Black criminals acted as if crime was a recreational sport. Congress had no choice.

We constantly insult each other in restaurants, on busses, etc. even when non-Blacks are there. The conversation of many young and even middle aged Blacks are limited to the words nigger, bitch, m----- f-----, ho, s—t, mixed in with a few verbs and nouns. If a white person says nigger then we pretend that we're offended. A white person can use the word nigger as long as they're a Democratic party official. Senator Robert Byrd of West Virginia and Cruz Bustamonte, the former Lt. Governor of California both used the word nigger but nobody complained. In Bustamonte's case he said it in front of a group of Black people. Insults must be confronted regardless of the political association of the offender.

Most of us really don't care anyway. Our outrage is just for show. We should not be the fools of America and the world. We are we the only people on Earth who spend vast fortunes yet own nothing. In political terms the Republicans ignore us and Democrats take us for granted. This is not about Democrats or Republicans. This is about our future and us. The Company will not be interested in politics. If we gain real economic power, they'll come to us.

You must remember that sometimes people give terrible advice to you. When I was in junior high school my guidance counselor told me to drop academics and concentrate on vocational studies. I refused. I wasn't a great student but I was adequate so why should I change my path. I remember the movie Malcolm X starring Denzel Washington. In the movie the teacher tells Malcolm to give up his dream of being an accountant. A white friend of mine who taught math in the West Hempstead New York told me that Black children were packed into special education classes no matter how smart they were. I know a Black female who was told to drop out of high school by her guidance counselor. She's a college graduate now.

That reminds me of South Africa's apartheid government's attempt to ban a song by the British rock group Pink Floyd called The Wall. The Wall was about indoctrination of children. The main phrase from the songs is "we don't need no education, we don't need no thought control". The teachers realize that a lot of Black parents are indifferent to their child's education and act accordingly. After all why should they care if Black kids don't want to learn, as teachers, they're going to get paid anyway.

If we do not change there will be no future. Racists always say the Black man has no future. Let's prove them wrong. As a great American philosopher, Yogi Berra, once said, "it ain't over til it's over".

Peonage

In J. W. Smith's Economic Democracy: The Political Struggle for the 21ˢᵗ Century peonage is described as follows: "In classic peonage, workers, though nominally free and legally free are held in servitude by the terms of their indenture to their masters. Because their wages are too low, the master grants credit but restricts the worker to buy overpriced goods from the master's own store. As a result, each month the peon goes deeper and deeper into debt".

Is that not the situation in the Black community now?

We have enormous potential. Our culture is marketable. But the first step is to be honest about the problems we have in the community. For some this will be a challenge.

In my opinion these are some of the major problems of the African American community:

We spend a lot of money but we own nothing
The behavior of some of our people is terrible
Our academic performance is the worst of any ethnic group
The Black family has been torn apart
Parents are ignoring their children, not teaching them proper values or stressing education
We refuse to trade with our people in America, Africa, Brazil, the Caribbean, etc.
Single female headed households are killing us
"Bad Boy" Black men are being crippled by females who cater to weak males
Morbid obesity among our females and young children will result in early diseases and deaths
We are dealing with an extremely racist media, which has learned to buy off some of our no talent "entertainers" and promote them as stars. In return they must denigrate our race.
A severe lack of pride and strong self hatred
The Company will honestly address each of theses problems.

The major strengths of the African American community are:

We have an annual income of approximately $662,000,000,000.00

We have millions of educated people
Most Americans are in fact friendly towards us
We have a marketable culture
Africa is a vast treasure house
There are millions of our people in Brazil and the Caribbean

The Company believes it has a workable plan to attack the major problems of the African American community.

There's only one way for us to prosper. We have to take control of our spending. Right now we almost give our money away. For your $10 you may get a bucket of chicken but that's all your getting. In other communities not only would you get the bucket of chicken, but also the store where you bought it will help make you richer. Usually money turns over several times. For instance, that $10 should turn into $80 or more before leaving the neighborhood. The retailer, the trucking companies, the chicken wholesaler, etc. all get a portion of that $10. I'll get back to the bucket of chicken later.

I Remember You

Last year when one of my friends was visiting in North Carolina he stopped at the local Food Lion supermarket. As he stepped out of the side of his car a young man approached him and asked for a dollar. It was in the evening but he recognized a resemblance to the family that had once owned the very property the supermarket and mini-mall was on. He asked the young man, didn't your family own this property at one time? He replied 'yes'. Then he proceeded to tell my friend how his family had been cheated out of the property with unpaid secured loans and tax liens.

When asked 'how could this happen? He replied, we didn't know that it could be taken that way. The property is now worth between $15 and $20 million dollars. My friend has told me that he's heard young Blacks lament about not getting paid for educational accomplishments. He tells them, 'you may not get paid for what you know, but what you don't know will cost you'. His point is that generational wealth in the Black community is being lost every day because the next generation is not informed on how to retain family homes, family farms and businesses. This is a direct result of the lack of knowledge in general and legal matters and business matters in particular.

Merchants in our community hire a lot of people but they don't hire our people. That's fine. We'll hire ourselves. All we need to do is for a small percentage of us to stick together. We cannot fail because we're competing against zero "0". The Company will directly attack this weakness. Every day you see young Black males on corners just hanging out. They and all of us are victims of our current beliefs and habits. We must change. We can be rich. We've done it before. The used to be a thriving Black business community in Tulsa Oklahoma. Many of you have heard of the Black Wall Street that was located in Tulsa. We had 21 restaurants, 30 grocery stores, our own movie houses, and over 600 other businesses. Do you see that now? No! Imagine 30 grocery stores in a small town like Tulsa decades ago.

None of our current "leaders" will even mention what we had because if we become successful then they might have to get a real job. The reason we were so rich in Tulsa is that a dollar spent by a Black person circulated dozens and sometimes hundreds of times before leaving the community. This flow of cash is called the Economic Multiplier. I will discuss The Multiplier later. Now a dollar leaves the area in less than an hour. As everyone knows, success creates jealousy, the green monster that we've all seen. It must be served. The Ku Klux Klan, white business interests and poor whites in Tulsa conspired to burn it all down. They also murdered over 3,000 Black people. An excellent source of information is "Black Wall Street: A Lost Dream".

The Company definitely intends to build a new Black economic empire.

We are much more powerful now but our power is potential, not kinetic. Kinetic power is power that is being used. Potential power is power that is not being used. Potential power is like George Foreman sleeping. Kinetic power is like Big George landing a big one on you. The Company intends to turn our potential power into kinetic power. If we combine just a small percentage of our kinetic power we can be great.

The terrible behavior of some of our people is causing us great harm. Cursing, being obnoxious, disrespectful, etc. is destroying our credibility. It's one thing to have a conversation in private with your friends and something else to be in public and saying the same things. Isn't it hypocritical for people who curse at home or among their friends and not to curse in public? Yes it is, but hypocrisy is the basis of civilization. We can't succumb to our base instincts.

Man is a savage, but must act civilized in order to survive. We cannot afford to have bad manners. Not just to appeal to others but to feel proud ourselves. The Company will try to make it profitable for our people to exhibit character, honor and knowledge. Black Americans had the lowest SAT scores of any ethnic group in 2003. Lower than Mexican Americans, Puerto Ricans, Asians, Whites, everybody! Knowledge has no status in our community. The Company will attempt to change that. The Company will seek out and train young people to be future business owners. We will seek out good students.

The Company's attitude with the young will be, "It's not where you start, and it's where you finish". The Company will encourage parents and grandparents to open investment accounts for the young. These young people will be given the same respect as adult investors. We need to show the advantages of being smart.

Speaking of being smart, we have to make the parties complete for our vote. Right now most Black people will vote Democratic no matter what. This has to be the dumbest addiction in the USA. Black people are saying all the time that the Democratic Party takes our vote for granted. Of course they take us for granted. If you can get somebody's vote by just smiling and grinning why not take him or her for granted. Just like any relationship, even romantic ones, being taken for granted is a sure sign of weakness.

What would happen if Blacks gave 40% of their votes to the Republicans just once? You would see a big change in the way the Democrats deal with Blacks. It's simple mathematics. The Democrats haven't got the majority of the white vote since 1964. They cannot win without the Black vote, period. If Republicans begin to get a larger share of the Black vote the Democrats would respect us. They'd abandon the "leadership" and go to the masses. They would have to offer us something real instead of what we get now, which is nothing. All Democrats do now is cater to the Uncle Toms who worship their whiteness while pretending they care for the people. Any white politician who says he respects the Black "leadership" is a racist or a liar. It's impossible to respect people who abandon their people for a career as an 'activist'. Living large and thinking small.

Let's engage in a little fantasy. Suppose a group of Blacks came up with an agenda and took it to both major parties. Let's say they wanted a tax credit maximum of $2,000 per year for 10 years for descendants of American slaves only. Africans, Hispanics, gays, non-Black women and other national subgroups would not be eligible for the credit. Let's also suppose that the $2,000 had to be invested in African American owned businesses, the Caribbean or Africa. Let's pretend that both parties looked at the plan. The party that backs our economic agenda should get our vote. The current "leaderships" agenda is themselves and their friends. Except for Louis Farrakhan they're not even asking Black people to band together and help themselves.

Affirmative action and set-asides are not going to get us where we want to go. Neither is begging. A few years ago a Black actor was in the paper because he complained that cab drivers wouldn't pick him up in New York. He arranged a meeting with the taxi drivers' representative to discuss the issue. At the end of the meeting a reporter asked the head of the taxi drivers' organization was this a case of racism. Her reply was "we're part of the community aren't we" or something to that affect. In other words everybody discriminates against Blacks so we're doing it also.

For Black people this was what Winston Churchill called an "unmitigated defeat". Churchill was speaking about the backstabbing deal the French (what else is new) and Britain signed with Hitler. The deal gave away part of Czechoslovakia without even consulting them. The French seem to specialize in backstabbing. When Nasser of Egypt became the first Egyptian since 600 BC to rule Egypt he seized the Suez Canal. France, Israel and Britain took the Canal from Egypt. The United States and The Soviet Union made them give it back. I've even read that the French are hostile to African Americans when they visit Africa.

There's no way in hell we should be begging people to take our money. Ironically this same woman was upset after 9/11 because many of the taxi drivers she represented were from Muslim countries and she was complaining about discrimination. She should be advocating for women's rights in Muslim countries like Afghanistan were females weren't allowed to go school and were beaten in the streets in broad daylight.

What the actor should have done is petition the city to allow special cabs that will pick up Blacks to operate in the City. Black Americans are conditioned to beg. I'll give you a specific example. In New York's Black areas most of the cab and van drivers are Africans or West Indians. Black Americans would never get the idea or have the drive to do this. They would rather complain to the city about service. In New York City there are very few Black American restaurants because we don't invest. Most of the Black ones that do exist are West Indian. We must regain our drive.

The Company will set up an infrastructure for the young that will nurture their ambitions and dreams. Right now most young Blacks don't see anything happening in their community that's encouraging. They see rappers and athlete's making a lot of money but they don't see businessmen and women succeeding. Of course there's many Blacks who are making it in business but almost all work for white companies.

They might as well be on the moon because Black youth don't see them. They work where Black youngsters never go. They usually live where they never go.

You can't blame the successful Blacks for leaving the community because it's dangerous to live there. Young people have to be challenged on their positive side. Black people have to use their gray matter instead of what we're doing now.

Our community accepts low academic standards. Parents are not pushing their kids to excel. Terrible test scores are blamed on the schools, lack of money from the government, etc. The real responsibility is the parents but many just don't care.

Below is the SAT performance chart for 2003 by ethnic group. Read it and weep.

SAT Chart

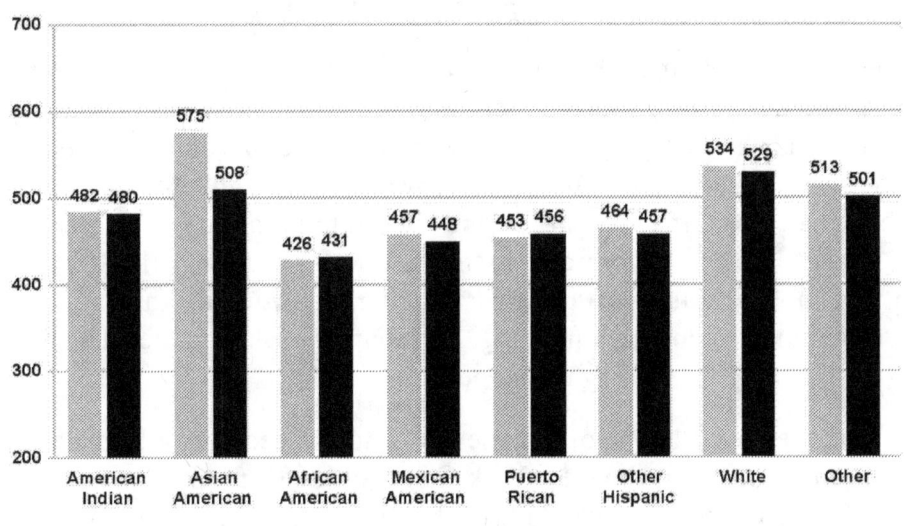

Graph 10:
SAT Scores Vary by Race/Ethnicity
(Data for SAT Takers in the Class of 2003)

The Black Family

The Black family has been destroyed on purpose. The usual suspects are at work. We are in an economic trap. If you study the history of warfare you will see how nations are conquered. Even in boxing they say if you kill the body the head will die. If an army moves in to destroy an enemy they only goes after the males. Females and children are of no consequence to a conquering army. That's why the normal Black males had to be eliminated in terms of power and influence in their families.

How does that relate to the breakup of the Black family? In the 60's Blacks were united and moving up. Those who now exploit us realized that our income would be greatly increasing. They would not be able to burn us out like they did in the Tulsa Oklahoma years ago. A new more sophisticated strategy evolved.

We were on a roll. Our current masters realized that the Black man was going to rise. The strategy was to weaken the Black social structure in order to control us. A young Patrick Moynihan warned us what was coming. Mr. Moynihan later became a United States Senator from the state of New York. Of course he was called a racist for telling the truth. Every strength we had was turned against us and is used to humiliate us today. The best way to weaken the Black race was to break up the families. Providing Black females with constant praise, free money, housing, furniture and better opportunities than males did this. In return she was required to do only one thing, humiliate the Black male. This is exactly what happened.

As a young Black female told one of my friends "I don't need you, all I need is Mr. Sugarman". Mr. Sugarman was the New York City Welfare Commissioner. Now after decades of encouraging women to depend on welfare these same forces are using them as targets. They were saying "there's so many Black people on welfare" but they forgot that Blacks are a minority on welfare. Even in New York City most of the people on welfare are not Black. So naturally they toned their rhetoric down.

The damage had already been done.

Economically the entire Black community is on welfare. If white people decided not to employ us we would starve. We can't provide jobs for ourselves and no other ethnic group besides whites will hire us.

Also in the 70's a new phrase was being uttered, "the Black man ain't nothing". At the same time the phrase "strong Black woman" came into fashion. It was and is a trick. If the Black man "wasn't nothing" starting in the 70's he really must have been nothing before that. Before the 70's Black women never said that. This is an example of what Don King calls trickeration. All of a sudden Black women were saying this to Black men. Black females have personally insulted almost every normal Black male.

Two Black females told me on the New York City subway "I don't know why you're wearing a suit, you know you only work in the mailroom". I found this comment curious for two reasons. First of all, what's wrong with working in the mailroom? Black women should remember that old country saying, "you have to dance with the one that brung ya". Working in a mailroom is honest work, so why should it be an object of derision. At that time I had my degree in Economics and Business from Fordham University and I was engaged in designing and implementing an advanced financial system. The system, Financial Information Reporting at Equitable, contained hundred of thousands accounts and balanced over $30,000,000,000.00 to the penny every day.

I was also a veteran of the United States Air Force. An associate of mine, a computer expert with a Master's in Finance and has designed databases was asked by 2 Black females why he had a briefcase because "ain't nothing in it except your lunch".

In the business district of major cities today Black males don't dare look at Black females. They know that if their eyes meet hers she will automatically turn her nose up and look the other way. Black males will acknowledge each other but most Black females act as if they're offended that a Negro mistook them for Black and cast his lowly eyes on them. This is especially true if they have a wig on. If the wig is blond then you're really in trouble. Other people, men or women do not do that to Black males. Black males would rather go to hell than look at a Black female in business districts. The result is that many working Black males never socialize with Black females in downtown business districts. Of course there are exceptions but in general this is true. Non-Black women are taking advantage of this. They don't mind a working Black man.

All you have to do is go to a restaurant in a downtown area. There are usually several tables with just Black females alone. Most of the Black males in these places are with non-Black females. This is especially true with young Black males. Although not a scientific observation I once counted the number of couples with a Black member in New York City at Broadway and 53rd Street. I counted 23 mixed couples over 2 hours. There were 2 totally Black couples. There were 21 couples where one of the pair was a Black male and the other person a non-Black female. The females in these couples were not just white. There were Chinese and Hispanic females with Black males also. I asked one Black male why was he with an Asian woman and he said "survival".

This is a serious problem. The Black males who are working and in college must be the ones females should approach but this is not happening. Criminals and "bad boys" are given priority by many Black females. The social work/welfare establishment encouraged Black females to have children as often as possible regardless of the character of the fathers and now the chickens are coming home to roost.

Black women were told you could get rent, food, etc. for nothing; however, you must get rid of your man. This was the deathblow of the Black family. Black females were also given preferences in jobs for obvious reasons. If you were the boss whom would you hire?, a male or an attractive female. Most bosses are males. Go figure.

Parents are not teaching their children the importance of being a good human being. This has nothing to do with race. The Company plans to provide a mechanism that will illustrate the advantages of being polite, knowledgeable and prideful. The Company will encourage the young to be honorable. Nobody can force anybody to do anything but people can be made to see that's in their interest to behave in a positive manner. Black youth today are encouraged by the entertainment industry to be uncivilized. If being a nigga, a ho or a bitch will get you a recording contract then people are going to do it. Children can be manipulated very easily. Look at how the Ku Klux Klan and Nazi Germany indoctrinated children into becoming monsters.

Africa is the key to our future. Our relationship with Africa is stupid. If we were Chinese Americans we would be trading with China. As I said before, we can be rich. We can hire Africans for $1 an hour and increase their incomes in many cases at least 8 times over. We can be heroes to Africans, the people of the Caribbean and Brazilians. As much money as we spend we all should be rich. Black people do not even know that many BMW's, Mercedes Benz's and Volkswagens are made in Rosslyn, South Africa. Ignorance is very dangerous. It allows others to keep you in bondage. As Louis Farrakhan has said, "a slave can't free anybody".

I know that this is a hot topic but it cannot be ignored because without change in childbearing practices, we are doomed. Black females have to change their behavior. It is the pinnacle of irresponsibility to have children out of wedlock today. It's even worse because it's occurring on a mass scale. 64% of Black girls between 13 and 19 will get pregnant. This is killing us. There are several problems with what's happening.

(A) The mother usually hasn't completely her education and/or job experience cycle. This means she cannot financially support her offspring without help.

(B) She hasn't got a committed partner to help her.

(C) Children growing up without a father are at a disadvantage. Males are several times more likely to end up in prison. Girls are more likely to get pregnant. The presence of a responsible male will decrease this ratio.

(D) Today's stressful lifestyle can overwhelm a single mother. Many can't possibly cope with all the duties of working and raising a child properly by themselves. If they were married they would have a partner to relieve her and she could enjoy a better life.

(E) Even if she has completed her education she's propelled right back down by having babies out of wedlock because today 1 parent usually cannot cope.

The Fall of the Black Male

Decades ago there were 133,226 Blacks in prisons. Now the total is approaching 1,000,000. That's an increase of 750%. This is a disaster. 1 in 10 Black men are in prison. Blacks make up 50% of the national prison population. There are more Blacks in prison than the population of 29 states. Felons can't vote in many states. Forget about getting a good job. I've seen brothers do things publicly that I can't even put in this book. We're failing everywhere.

Take Washington State for example.

	Population Percentage	Prison Percentage
Blacks	3.4%	23%
Native Americans	1.9%	3.2%
Hispanic	6%	13%

As you can see the other minorities are in prison at a rate of about twice their population percentage. Blacks are in prison at 767% more than their population percentage. Racism is not the cause, it's our criminal culture and our tactics.

What happened?

We've been had. It happens to everybody at some point in his or her life. In our case it happened to millions at once. Young Black males are encouraged to be immoral by popular culture. Cursing athletes, publicly decadent behavior, vulgar music and worse. Young Blacks don't see anything positive in their lives. The only people they see succeeding are athletes and entertainers and drug dealers. It's not totally their fault that many of them are growing up ignorant and uncivilized.

They're victims. President Reagan went to a German military cemetery and it caused a small controversy. People said the cemetery was full of killers since some SS were buried there. But President Reagan said they were victims and he was right. German youth were indoctrinated to be inhuman from the moment the Nazi Party took power in 1933 until they were defeated in 1945. This is what is happening to us. We are being encouraged to be inhuman. Why would anyone want to debase Black people?

It's the two usual suspects, money and racism. There are trillions of dollars being made off Black buying power. We're the perfect costumer (suckers). We buy and we don't compete, challenge or even notice we're being economically raped. In order to rape the community you have to get the male out of the picture. Any army that has conquered a foe has eliminated the power of the males. Females and children are easy to handle. Blacks are facing a new more sophisticated racist than in the past. The new racists smile in you face and see only dollar signs. Since our "leadership" has lain down it's easy to rape the community.

The Black "leadership" has no real power. They're not respected at all. For example: a major civil rights organization chose a new leader a few years ago. This new leader wanted to be inclusive when it came to working with others in the Black community. The new leader made the mistake of wanting to work with another real man, Louis Farrakhan. Non-Black forces quickly gathered and demanded that the new leader break contact with the real man. The new leader was a real man himself and a struggle ensued. The non-Black outsiders won and the new leader was dismissed. I heard they replaced him with a boy.

"The Black male is an endangered species" has almost become a cliché. It's true. The Black male has to ignore the current "leadership" and others. Our enemies, those I call smiling Nazis have convinced many Black females that if the males go extinct they'll still be around. Sisters don't you believe it! We must have our own agenda. Black people have been taught to dislike each other. This was the method of controlling slaves on the plantation. If you can divide people by sex, age, status, skin color, etc. you can maintain control. This has been tried all over the world throughout human history. A lot of the times it's very effective. In India for example, they have the caste system.

The Black community is not taking advantage of the vast expertise and experience base that it has. Even if every white person in the United States acted like Jesus Christ the Black community would not change that much. Why? Because Black people will have to change their habits and beliefs in order to improve our condition. Some white people can help, especially males who can assist in redirecting Black male youths. White industrialists are also very valuable.

Even if a Black criminal decides to go straight he's going to find that he has little chance of making it legally. What opportunities are there in the Black community? If you fall out of the white economy you may never recover. A lot of us are just a few checks from welfare and/or even homelessness. It happened to me twice. I ended up on welfare after being laid off and I know many others that were unfortunate enough for this to happen to them. The Black community does not have an economic base that can provide jobs for our people.

The reason some Black males act in a destructive manner is because they can't really be a full man. How can you be a man when you can't support yourself, can't take care of your lady and children, lack self-esteem and can't look normal men in the eye. That's why some many Black males indulge in destructive behavior. Many resort to baby making as proof of their manhood. This is an example of a "Weapon of Mass Distraction". The Weapons are designed to make you believe you're accomplishing or knowing something when in reality you're being exploited.

Take the car business. All Americans love a hog. Big cars are great but the problem is that we don't own any of the car dealerships. They want us to be purely customers. Our masters want to keep Blacks, especially males from starting businesses.

If Blacks got into starting their own businesses then our youth will begin to gain self-esteem, crime would drop, people would be more respectful and we would prosper. That is the nightmare of the merchants in our community who take and never give. It is also the worst nightmare of the smiling Nazis would control our leadership and the media. Black people are not poor, that's just something that's often repeated to keep us passive and discouraged. "The white man ain't gonna let us do anything" is the phrase often used by brainwashed Blacks when you mention self-determination.

The white man isn't thinking about us unless you're committing a crime. Why waste time thinking about somebody who'd rather whine and beg than try to improve his own life. The situation is dire but can be overcome with will.

I know a lot of our people will hate to hear this but our most dangerous enemy today is the Arab. Arabs insist on continuing the slave trade in Africa and are committing genocide right now against Black people in Africa. The Palestinian people were pushed off their land and they have a legitimate cause however the Arabs have to face up to their behavior regarding Black people. I think we should concentrate on Egypt as far as dealing with Arabs. They have more experience internationally and wisdom then the others. I don't put our people's interest second to anybody's.

Respect for elders has almost completely disappeared. Black men should remember the ancient proverb of the Masai of Kenya, "you're not a man until your father dies".

Brothers, we have to do our duty.

==

NOTES

The Fall of The Black Female

The biggest victims of the smiling Nazis are Black females. In March 2004 The Village Voice, a major New York Weekly featured an article by author Thulani Davis entitled "The Height of Disrespect". It has been obvious for many years that many Black females have discarded the concept of being respected. The value and respect for young Black females is zero in this new urban culture. It has now reached rock bottom. Every day you hear it from their own mouths, calling each other bitches and ho's in public and not even caring.

The Height of Disrespect highlights a recent study concerning African American households with income of less than $25,000. Girls in these households are getting pregnant at an alarming rate. Motivational Educational Entertainment of Philadelphia conducted the study. These are some of the names by which young Black males refer to Black females: Block bender, chicken head, skeezer, hood rat, bitch, ho, hoochie mama and others just as disrespectful.

2,000 teens in 80 communities based groups in 9 urban areas were involved in the study. The basic philosophy is "play or be played". Many of these young women cannot relate to a normal male. Any male who does not exploit them is considered a fool who can be fleeced. This has resulted in the most promising Black males dating non-Black women when they want a serious relationship. One of my Black female friends who resides in public housing in New York said that even in the hood Black males are seeking Hispanic women for serious relationships. This is also leading to homosexual relationships among Black females, especially dark skinned ones. Also we all know that many Black males will reject a dark skinned female no matter how pretty she is.

Young Black females are engaged in kamikaze behavior and they're taking the entire race down with them. When you see young girls with their babies you never see males with them. That should tell them something about the choices they're making. In 2001 African American adults and young people has an AIDS case rate 10 that of whites. Black females from 13 to 19 represent 66% of AIDS cases among young women. Black youths have had an average of 4 or more sex partners by age 13.

Black females have become accustomed to being disrespected. Many actually seek out "bad boys" for relationships. It's common to know of or hear of educated Black females having babies by criminals and non-working males. You can't really blame the men because males will always be attracted to sexually receptive females and MALES DON'T GET PREGNANT. The terrible decision by Black females to bear children by weak males is destroying the race. By "weak" I mean weak in terms of ethics, sincerity, honor and pride. Black females know these men are not going to assist them in rearing their children and yet they blame "the Black man" when they don't. You must be responsible for your actions yourself.

Once a young woman has a child out of wedlock she puts herself at a tremendous disadvantage. She has disqualified herself from being the wife of millions of males.

In the past when a young lady became pregnant the male responsible would marry them. This is what happened in the case of my parents. The community recognized the need for a child to have a mother and a father. A single mother has most likely she has interrupted her education and faces a life of struggle. The cost of living is so high now that even if she gets a job she can't make ends meet alone. She must have help from relatives or male friends. This means that she must press relatives and males for money for food, rent, telephone, etc. The result is that males lose respect for her. She must live in a catch 22 with a hard long difficult way out. A lot of them aren't going to recover, ever!

Mistakes are compounded when she continues to have more children. The children suffer also because there is no male example to relate to. Young males never learn that you're not supposed to curse in front of others, that fighting and crime are not cool and can be fatal. Some women can handle the responsibility alone but it's obvious most can't.

Black females have forgotten that old saying "Beware of Greeks bearing gifts",

If someone is lavishing praise upon you and scorn upon your brother you have to ask yourself, what is the motive for these positions? It can only be to divide and conquer.

Remember what Roman emperor Julius Caesar said in Shakespeare's epic as his best friend stabbed him in the back, "et tu Brute" (you too Brutus).

You know what *The Undisputed Truth* said about smiling faces. They tell lies. Their sophisticated strategy resulted in Black females exhibiting a hatred of normal Black men. She caters to "bad boys' and her male children in ways that make them weak. Bad boys and criminals are not required to be responsible in any manner. In fact the opposite is true. Normal men are discriminated against and weak men nurtured. You can see this in the bizarre behavior that has become standardized.

Actual cases that I personally know are true

A Dr. gets pregnant by a janitor who comes to work only when he feels like it

Suburban wife says "the Black man ain't nothing" while she's driving a new car, don't work and lives in a big house while her Black husband goes to work every day

An accountant with a Master's degree in accounting has 3 children by a drug dealer

A young woman leaves her husband and kids and marries a man in prison for murder

Two sisters are impregnated by the same man living with them and is of course not working

Middle age woman still waiting for her non-working boyfriend "big settlement" from disability after 6 years

A woman pays her boyfriends bills after selling her home and later finds him in her bed with another woman

Young girl has a baby because all her girlfriends have one

A woman asks a friend to cosign for a car loan, when he asks her why not ask her relatives she replies, "I asked my father but he doesn't want to lose everything he's got".

This kind of decision-making has become standard behavior for many Black females. It only encourages Black men to be irresponsible. In addition it repels normal men who would otherwise become a responsible partner for these women.

Trickeration

Earlier in the 20th Century there was a great Native American named Grey Owl. Grey Owl was a Canadian American Indian. Grey Owl became a best selling author of wilderness adventures. He went on a lecture tour of Britain. The British King and his family were in awe when Grey Owl told them tales of the wilderness at a private meeting. The present Queen, Elizabeth II was there along with her father, The King, to listen to Grey Owl. Grey Owl was a committed conservationist. He brought up many issues that most people never thought of at the time. He even lectured against fox hunting during a broadcast in London. Grey Owl was the toast of Europe.

There was only one problem; Grey Owl was not an Indian. Worse still, he was an Englishman. The public only found out when his wife dropped a dime on him in the paper. Grey Owl died right before the scandal broke so he didn't have to face the fact that his deception has been discovered. The Grey Owl story reminds us that anybody can be fooled. How could the British, including the royal family be tricked into thinking that one of their countrymen was an American Indian? Grey Owl was in the hospital and his makeup came off but people ignored it.

Don King has a name for it, "trickeration". People don't see you; they see the image you're presenting to them. That's why Grey Owl could fool everybody. His act was good and they believed it. Muhammad Ali trickerated George Foreman with his Rope A Dope strategy. Big George thought he was wearing Ali down but it was he who was being worn down.

Trickeration is what's going on in the Black community. The media has convinced Black people that material items can make up for a lack of pride, self-interest and confidence. They've convinced almost everybody else too. This has lead to brand name mania. What not kill for an iced tea? A young Black New York girl was murdered for one. After all, a bottle of iced is refreshing.

I've noticed 2 trends in advertising that is very subtle but deliberate. If you notice you almost never see beautiful Black women in commercials except for cars and beer. In addition, a lot of these Black women in ads for household products are overweight, especially in some industries. Check it out. Another thing that advertisers do is match dark skin males with light skin females when showing a Black couple. You never see a light skinned male with a dark Black female. What is the purpose of this? Black children in commercials are almost never dark skinned. Could it be a message to Black males that if you buy this product or service you'll get a beautiful light skinned female? Advertisers never do anything by accident. "I only drink very expensive brandy, I drive a Lexus, I have a pair of $250 sneakers, etc." These things are all nice to have but I think in many people they've become substitutes for self-esteem.

When it comes to spending we're like Pavlov's dogs. Pavlov's principles have been shown to apply to people also. The advertising industry is based upon it. Once a teacher conducted an experiment on a room full of white children. The teacher told the class that blue-eyed people were bad. The behavior of the children towards the blue-eyed children became discriminatory. This is trickeration. We see a commercial and we go crazy. Some of our people are so crazed they'll kill for trinkets. Other people are fooled too but we go overboard. The trickeration is on us. In the science fiction series Star Trek Mr. Spock said something that is very true. "After a time you may find that wanting something is more pleasurable than having it, it is not logical but it is often true". When that big car note comes many people have to wonder if it was worth it. Then we go and ask for jobs from people driving a Chevy or VWs.

We have to delay getting everything we want for a few years when we can really afford them. People who control us buy inexpensive cars until they can really afford a fancy machine. The problem is that others have trickerated us into not investing thereby leaving them in control. All this buying is not leading to employment and business opportunities for Black people.

We see success in material things and so does everyone else on Earth. However everyone else is trading with his or her own people. Others are draining our community of capital that could be used to enrich our people.

Often you read where someone is murdered for something as simple as a pair of sneakers. What makes up a pair of sneakers? Plastic, denim cloth, rubber and shoelaces are all there is to sneakers. Yet some of our people are so low on the self-esteem scale that sneakers are worth more than a Black person's life.

Think about the mentality that goes along with this behavior.

==

NOTES

It's Not Where You Start But Where You Finish

The richest man in the world used to work in McDonalds. That's right, Bill Gates, the Chairman of Microsoft worked at McDonalds. The very fact that you, as a young person, has a job gives you a completely different prospective on things. One of the big reasons our youth get into so much trouble is that there are no jobs for them in the community. We have to adopt a strategy that provides opportunities for Black youth to go down the straight and narrow.

I once heard a prominent Black woman put down people who cleaned other people's houses for a living. I objected to her stance. My beloved aunt who was my surrogate mother cleaned houses much of her life. There are millions of Black people who are what they are today because their mother or grandmother cleaned homes in order to help feed the family. Being a maid was a great job to have early in the last century. For a man a great job was being a Pullman porter on a train. "He was a man of his times", is heard quite often when discussing people and what they did in history. Many Black people today are not people of the 21st Century but people of the 19th Century. Our thinking today us super backward. Black people with good jobs seem to have a problem relating to other Blacks. If the Black race is going to advance the educated and prosperous Blacks must lead.

There are only 1,441 Black architects (1,281 males and 160 females) in the United States according to Blackarch.uc.com. If we begin to get our act together we will need a lot more. Since it takes a long time to educate an individual we will have to hire many non-Blacks. In fact many of the top managers in Company funded projects will be not be Black until Blacks catch up.

No group or nation on Earth can prosper without the help of other people. Take China for example. China's economy is growing at a very fast pace. Just look at the label on the things you buy. We are some of China's best customers. China cannot prosper without others buying their products. The Chinese will not prosper without American and other foreign experts designing their infrastructure. I personally believe that it would be easy to obtain the help Black people need to build our economic empire. Money will trump race. Look at the Jews. White people are always complaining to Black people about Jews yet the Jews are powerful. Why? People know that Jews can help them make money, it's just that simple. You don't have to show Blacks respect because you're going to get the money anyway.

Reagan's Contribution

President Reagan recently passed away and I like others watched his state funeral. The Black establishment did not like President Reagan. He wouldn't play their game. The situation was not good when President Reagan took office. National pride was down and inflation was up. Reagan made people believe that the best was yet to come. Psychology is every important when it comes to succeeding. It is also an important factor in failing also. Reagan provided hope and an end to a national shame. He ended inflation and gave the poor a great gift.

Optimism was Reagan's greatest strength. President Jimmy Carter is probably the most honorable man most of us have ever heard of. Unfortunately people sometimes take decency for weakness and that's what happened to President Carter during the Iranian hostage crisis. Hostages were held at the American Embassy in Teheran for over a year. A rescue attempt ended in disaster.

Mr. Carter had projected an image of being a flexible, honest and sincere man. The hostage takers misinterpreted this as weakness. I'm certain that if President Carter had been re-elected he would eventually have incinerated an Iranian city. The Iranians saw Reagan as a "cowboy" and everyone knows that you don't play with cowboys. On the day Reagan took office the Iranians let the hostages go. That ended a great national humiliation. Inflation was 15% when Reagan took office. While the word inflation seems benign it is actually a monster that can kill. Inflation was one of the reasons Hitler came to power in Germany. German inflation was unbelievable. A simple example based upon statistics from a 1970 study by Scientific Market Analysis illustrates the potential danger. Before the euro the German currency was the mark. For clarity let's suppose that the Germans were using the American dollar. Let's also suppose that that $1 dollar bought 1 pound of ground beef. This is how the prices changed in Germany over 9 years:

Date	Price of 1 pound of ground beef
July 1914	$1.00
January 1919	$2.60
July 1919	$3.40
January 1920	$12.60
January 1921	$14.40
July 1921	$14.30
January 1922	$36.70
July 1922	$100.60
January 1923	$2,785.00

July 1923 $194,000.00

November 1923 $726,000,000,000.00 for 1 pound of ground beef, imagine.

As strange as it looks it actually happened. This lead to political instability and the rise of Nazism as people became desperate for an end to chaos.

When Reagan left office inflation had been greatly reduced.

At one point in the 1970's the United States government instituted price controls to tame inflation. Reagan's gift to the poor was the Earned Income Tax Credit.

Ronald Reagan narrated the first documentary on the Tuskegee Airman that I ever saw. Richard Nixon was the President who started affirmative action or so I was told.

Nixon also looked out on the White Rose Garden and saw all the Black gardeners and said "get the niggers out of the Rose Garden, let's get Filipinos because we can work them to death". Communism in the Soviet Union lasted for decades before Russian patriots got sick of it and took a big chance to get rid of it. Communism looks great on paper but it ignores human nature, and therefore will never work. What we call liberalism has the same flaw. The Black leadership's strategy, whatever it is, is also brain dead. Nobody will respect people who whine about discrimination instead of competing.

Black people can't afford to continue with this defeatist ideology we have. The political class has abandoned our people here and in Africa, the Caribbean, Brazil, and other places with large number of Africans. We have to get back to what works. Blacks in America are the richest Africans in the world by far and yet we own nothing. Asking for reparations is not the answer; it keeps our focus off what we need to do.

We need the Boeings, the AT&T's, the IBM's, the Betchels, Dupont's, etc. of America. We need people like engineers, carpenters, and machinists, in other words, people who know how to do things; we've had our fill of talkers.

India

Why does the United States have the world's largest economy? Because it utilizes the talents of anybody from anywhere. If you look at future trends it's obvious what's going to happen. Many economists believe that India will eventually have an economy larger and richer than China's. I believe that Black people should do what the United States government is doing, that is, form a strategic alliance with East Indians. Why?

(1) India is producing highly educated people in quantity

(2) They come from a democracy

(3) They live in a lot of countries that have large Black populations. South Africa has over 1,000,000 Indians.

(4) They're very adaptable

AIDS is creating massive numbers of African children who are or will be orphans. Africa needs immigrants to adopt these children. African Americans are not going to move to Africa or adopt African children in large numbers. Africa also will need people to come and help to build the society. That's why the USA always took in immigrants. The African countries will have to do the same if they want to prosper. Of course there will have to be limitations.

Immigrants should be subject to certain economic controls to prevent immigrants from dominating the economy. Something like a restriction that says immigrants can own no more than 30% of a company. Their children who will be born in Africa can own 50% and their African born grandchildren 100% can own of a company. India will soon be the most populous country in the world. They do have one major problem, the terrible caste system. Therefore those at the bottom of the caste system, the untouchables, should be given priority. East Indians are generally friendly also. They were the only Asian ethnic group that gave the majority of their vote to David Dinkins when he ran for mayor of New York City.

A relatively small percentage of the African American population is all this is needed to succeed. A simple example proves this. Assume that there are 35,000,000 African Americans in the United States. If only 5% (1,750,000 people) of the African American population invests an average of $2,000 the first year, that's $3,5000,000,000. African Americans will never obtain investment and loans equal to that amount under the current strategy.

African Jerks

An economic plan has to have a rational goal and method of operation. African Americans in general do not know how to effectively run businesses, also when dealing with Africans we cannot afford to engage in romanticism. Two of the worse governments in Africa are those of Zimbabwe and Equatorial Guinea. Robert Mugabe of Zimbabwe and Obiang Nguem Mbasogo of Guinea are evil men. After over 20 years in office Mugabe "discovers" that white farmers control most of the best farmland. Where was his mind for 20 years before his "discovery"?

He was too busy being a dictator and corrupting the political system. For many years he's been on a mission to destroy the country. Even Nelson Mandela and Bishop Tutu are complaining about him. He's using the farmers in a desperate bid to stay in power. It is true that the land should be returned to Blacks because it was stolen from them.

Mugabe has allotted land to his cronies and supporters. Millions are on the verge of starvation because of his desire to stay in power. Why didn't he give the land to the farm workers or accept money from a fund set up to transfer the land back to Blacks? He uses murder and other means in order to lord over the nation.

The idiot that has ruled Guinea for over 20 years is even worse.

Oil has been discovered in Guinea and the potential wealth is enormous. Guinea has only 500,000 people but most live on less than $1 a day. Meanwhile this fool and his son were on CBS's 60 Minutes flying all over the world spending like drunken sailors. Riggs Bank in Washington DC has over $700 million in an account controlled by Mr. Mbasogo. His stupid son went to a fancy clothing store and bought 30 suits on 60 Minutes. If you assume that each suit costs $750 that's $22,500. It would take over 61 years for the average Guinean to earn $22,500. This is a country with no bookstores and only 4,000 televisions. Good governance has to be in place before we would invest in any country.

There are no insurmountable obstacles. The loans have to be based on a strategy to make Africans worldwide more self-sufficient. The only people that are totally self-sufficient are poor isolated tribes in various parts of the world. Another goal would be to ensure the companies THAT WE SELECT to work with us make a healthy profit. The loans should range from micro-loans for poor Africans to very large joint venture investments in businesses such as energy, auto manufacturing, etc.

Since Black people are behind many projects will be joint ventures and franchises. Currently successful small Black businesses will also be built up. Of course most of the investments will be for new start up businesses. Boeing will obtain our airplane orders because African Americans cannot influence Airbus if something is not right. We will work with those we need in the world but our interests always will come first.

Only a private company can implement a workable financial plan because once the government gets involved, the plan will be will bastardized and be inefficient. That's what happened with affirmative action. Affirmative action was started to try to address problems associated with the descendents of former slaves in America only. Affirmative Action has been bastardized to the extent that everybody in the country who is not a healthy Christian white male between 18 and 65 is eligible.

Weapons of Mass Distraction

American Idol, James Brown, Kobe Bryant, Supreme Court Law Clerks, Michael Jackson, O.J. Simpson, Clarence Thomas, etc.

I believe Tavis Smiley came up with the weapons of mass distraction phrase. Our masters can launch their Weapons of Mass Distraction at any time against our race. They control the media and therefore they control how most people think. Advertising works. The media has an extremely anti-Black agenda. Their agenda is to promote social change they chose to promote while at the same time highlighting Blacks misdeeds or even accusations.

The smartest person on television in the last 2 decades was Alan Keyes. Dr. Keyes was the only person on TV who actually had knowledge of what was going on. Of course he had to go. BET got rid of Tavis Smiley also. Often on "news" programs you will observe that the hosts are totally ignorant of history and current events. The people you see are just news "readers". That's why they light up during the entertainment portion of the news. They can handle that. The Company has a plan for establishing our own media.

Police nationwide have learned that you can make your career by bringing down or humiliating a famous Black person. It is true in some cases the Black person invites trouble by their behavior. The problem is that sometimes the person is just accused and even innocent. Sometimes it's just a new type of race baiting. It's not in the economic interest of the media to be fair concerning Black people. The media loves to play the race game.

Blacks have been in a huff because a Black favorite was voted off the American Idol. Elton John said it was racist and it was on the news. American Idol is irrelevant. This is nothing. Anybody who gets on the show is lucky. At least people got to see them.

This is a classic case of race baiting. Let's concentrate on creating and marketing our own new stars, The Company has a plan. By the way Elton John was once Patti LaBelle's piano player in Europe.

I looked on the Internet and here was this now famous picture of James Brown. The same picture that they took of him when he was arrested in a domestic dispute. Of course they took a picture of him when his hair was disheveled. What was strange about seeing the picture again a few weeks later was the reason for featuring the photo. It seems James Brown's wife quit his tour. Is this news? Is this a justifiable reason the feature the photo of Mr. Brown unkempt? It's just another Weapon of Mass Distraction.

Kobe Bryant and Michael Jackson haven't been convicted of anything. Personally I believe there are serious doubts about these cases. Why pretend Michael Jackson is a risk to flee when he's the most famous person on Earth. I'm not a fan of Mike Tyson's behavior but I have serious doubts about his guilt in the rape case he went to prison for.

It appears the media needs these Weapons of Mass Distraction to shield their social change agenda from the American public. A couple of years ago there was word in the Black community about there being no Black Law Clerks at The Supreme Court. This is stupid. Even if every Justice on the Court had a Black Law Clerk that would only be 9 jobs. There are millions of Blacks underemployed or unemployed. Recently in a survey of young people they were asked the if they could name the Supreme Court Justices, most could not even name one, not even Clarence Thomas. Most of these young people were white. This ignorance problem is not just a Black problem.

The O. J. Industry is fighting for survival but they are having a hard time. They refuse to tell the American people the real reason O.J. was found not guilty. The prosecution could not discredit O.J's chief witness, Dr. Henry Lee. The samples of O.J's blood collected at the crime scene contained a preservative. Preservatives do not occur naturally in the body, which means the police planted the blood evidence they "found". In addition Dr. Lee pointed out that the killer would be a bloody mess. The media have tried several times to intimidate Dr. Lee into saying OJ did it but Dr. Lee always says he just goes by the science. To show how unprincipled the media is, a network actually employs the nincompoop Geraldo Rivera, the lowest form of life on Earth. As an illustration of his lack of character he wrote a book telling of sexual encounters with women whom he named. Some of these women were by then married but he obviously doesn't care about anything except making a buck. Back to OJ, Geraldo's favorite subject. You just can't wash blood off your body quickly. Enzymes would be on O.J. and in the pipes at his home. The police took the pipes from his home and found nothing. I say again O.J. got off because of science.

The Black establishment is wrongly persecuting Clarence Thomas. What is Justice Thomas doing that's hurting Black people? Is he selling crack or robbing anybody, calling our women bitches and ho's, etc. The reason they dislike him is because their masters instructed them to. Their masters don't want any Black to escape the plantation. A poll of Blacks was taken during Judge Thomas' confirmation and it found that a majority of Blacks supported him. I read where a civil rights organization said Blacks didn't understand the issues. I suspect that Justice Thomas' dark skin plays a role in their hatred. It's just the impact of another Weapon of Mass Destruction. The smiling Nazis of the media are very sophisticated in their racist tactics and they're very clever in disguising it. Presidents Clinton and Bush Jr. took weeklong trips to Africa. Did you notice anything missing about media coverage of their trips? I notice that even though they went to very large sophisticated cities NOT 1 BUILDING WAS EVER SHOWN ON THE TELEVISION. The effect was that it presented an image that said that Africa was one gigantic zoo. This was not accidental. There's a method to their racism.

Phil Specter and Robert Blake

The weapons that should be launched

Phil Specter and Robert Blake are both accused of capital murder. Both are very famous people yet the media is silent. Why, because they're not Black (and other reasons). So what if they're accused of more serious crimes than Kobe or Michael. The media is not interested in them, they're not Black. Nuff said.

===

NOTES

Adam Smith and The Invisible Hand

In 1776 an Englishman named Adam Smith published a book called The Wealth of Nations. Adam Smith is generally regarded as the father of economics. The most quoted paragraph in the book concerns the "invisible hand". I've included it here and I will give my analysis on the use of the invisible hand in the Black world.

"every individual necessarily labours to increase the annual revenue of the society as great as he can. He generally, indeed, neither intends to promote the public interest, nor knows how much he is promoting it.

By preferring the support of domestic to that of foreign industry, he intends his own security; and by directing that industry in such a manner as its produce may be of the greatest value, he intends his own gain and he is in this, as in many other cases, led by an invisible hand to promote an end which was no part of his intention. Nor is it always the worse for the society that it was no part of it.

By pursuing his own interest he frequently promotes that of the society more effectually then when he really intends to promote it.

I have never known much good done by those who affected to trade for the public good"

Adam Smith

The Wealth of Nations, 1776

The Black Race and The Invisible Hand

The "invisible hand" is not working in the Black community. Our "leadership" structure is not geared to benefit the vast majority of our people. Black people are NOT ECONOMICALLY SELFISH ENOUGH. Black people believe in instant gratification. Instant gratification means poverty and weakness in the long run. In the case of the Black race it may lead to extinction.

Let's look at what Adam Smith is saying. *"every individual necessarily labours to increase the revenue of the society as great as he can. He generally, indeed, neither intends to promote the public interest, nor knows how much he is promoting it"*.

Everybody should be acting in his or her own economic interest. If you do your best to help yourself then the society will prosper because of your efforts. If you open a restaurant then you're helping everybody. The business will need employees, suppliers and other services. This adds to the wealth of the community. Your intention may be to get rich but that doesn't matter as long as you're productive. Black people have been indoctrinated into not being productive. We've been trained to beg. Our "leaders" can't encourage real economic development because their masters might cut of the money. The job they have is to deliver our money to the Massa.

"By preferring the support of domestic to that of foreign industry, he intends his own security; and by directing that industry in such a manner as its produce may be of the greatest value, he intends his own gain and he is in this, as in many other cases"

This is the major economic problem in the Black community. Most Blacks don't want to deal with other Blacks and most Black business people don't want to respect their customers. In this case the *"foreign industry"* is the businesses owned by non-Blacks in our community. The *"foreign industry"* takes billions of dollars out of our community and contributes nothing. If you notice the *"foreign industry"* never employs Black people. One thing I will say about white people is that they could ALWAYS find people in the community to employ when they owned these businesses. By not developing an internal economic infrastructure the Black community is committing suicide.

Most Black business people have a very bad attitude towards the community. Almost everybody has experienced inferior service from Black people they have hired. Often people have to call a white man to finish the task correctly. I've experienced this attitude personally when I took over a fruit stand for a couple of weeks. In just 1 week I tripled the gross of the stand by just greeting people with a smile and treating them with respect. The owner of the property pulled me aside and said not to greet them and that I should "make them come to you".

I felt this was a stupid way to do business since they were giving me money for watermelons, cantaloupes, and other items they were buying. After he saw my technique was working he wanted to be my partner instead of renting the place to me. I was going to pay him twice the rent he had before. No, he wanted to be my partner. Needless to say I left.

"By pursuing his own interest he frequently promotes that of the society more effectually then when he really intends to promote it." The reason groups or nations become wealthy is because individuals start businesses that prosper. Starting a business is the best antipoverty program there is. Nothing the government can do can lead to long- term prosperity better than community based businesses. The businessperson is following a dream or seeking wealth, so what, their efforts will benefit everybody.

It's on now.

===

NOTES

Statistical Facts About The African American Community

According to the United State's Census Bureau's 2002 Current Population Survey (CPS) There were 35,803,000 Black people in the United States at that time.
Blacks make up 13% of the American people.
The 2002 CPS also said that the Per Capita Income (CPI) for Blacks in 2002 was $15,441. Many people will misinterpret a CPI. The CPI means that all Blacks are included in it. This means that babies, teenagers, the elderly retired, prisoners, workers and youngsters are all used in this calculation.
If you multiply the CPS Black population estimate (35,803,000) times the CPI ($15,441) you'll get the total income for Blacks in 2002.
The total income for Blacks in America for the year 2002 was $552,880,446,000.00.

If we were a separate country we'd be in the top 15. That's more than all of Africa put together. The problem is that all this money is not leading to greater wealth for our people. It's not helping inner city kids find a job. It's not helping Black Colleges raise the funds they need. It's not helping ex-offenders clean up their lives and become productive citizens instead of a menace. The Company will change things.

There are certain things we should be doing that were not doing. Not only should we be trading with each other we should be trading with Africa, Brazil, and the Caribbean.

There's gold in them thar hills.

Southern Africa is so rich in natural resources that instruments on airplanes are affected when they fly over it. There is a vast labor supply. We can employ an African for $1 per hour and he'd be a rich man in some countries. This also would create a market for African American produced products. As the African societies gradually become more prosperous enormous opportunities will become common. The Company has a plan.
According to the 2002 CPS 27% of Black married couples earn more than $75,000 per year. This statistic alone illustrates the benefit of a stable relationship between a man and a woman. 52% of Black married couples had an annual income of $50,000 or more. Yet 58% of Black families had an annual income of less than $25,000 in 2002. Single parent households are very vulnerable.
There were 8,800,000 Black families in 2002. 48% were married couples. This compares to 82% for the white population. 43% were female-headed households compared to 13% for whites. The high female-headed household percentage is our biggest weakness. This is not about who's perfect and who's not. Nobody is perfect so that's the end of that discussion. This is about serious problems that must be addressed.

People are not animals where once the eggs are hatched everybody goes their separate ways. Children need a mother and a father. In earlier years the men of a town could guide young males. Now the community doesn't produce uncles and others who could take a young man under his wing. Black females have to start making better decisions concerning child bearing. A person's character is very important. Obviously qualities such as character and knowledge on the part of the fathers are insignificant.

The lack of a positive male influence in young Black's live is resulting in a total absence in self-respect. There are many women who are rearing top shelf people on their own. These kids still need a positive male influence. The Company will make sure that children are exposed to positive males. The Company will try to recruit males to be mentors. The Company believes a lot of Blacks, white and others would love to do it.

18% of Black Women and 16% of Black men have degrees at the bachelor's level or better. Why isn't this vast storehouse of knowledge, experience and creativity not being utilized to help the race overcome our problems? Because the powers that be in our community just don't care. They won't even come to us with a plan to help ourselves. The Company will seek out people with any kind of expertise. The Company has a plan. Lawyers, carpenters, architects, chefs, retired military, truck drivers, etc. will all be recruited by The Company. The Company has total confidence in Black people.

Statistical Facts about selected countries with Significant Black Populations

Source: 2003 CIA World Fact Book

South Africa
Gross Domestic Product: $432,000,000,000
Population: 42,768,678
Per Capita Income: $10,000

United States of America
Gross Domestic Product: $10,400,000,000,000 (Black, 2000 Census, $552,880,000,000)
Population: 290,342,554 (12.9% Black)
Per Capita Income: $36,300 (Black $15,441)

Haiti
Gross Domestic Product: $10,000,000,000
Population: 7,527,817
Per Capita Income: $1,400
(I saw in the paper that Haitians are now eating dirt to survive)

Nigeria
Gross Domestic Product; $112, 500,000,000
Population: 133,881,703
Per Capita Income: $900

Dominican Republic
Gross Domestic Product: $53,780,000,000
Population: 8,715,602 (73% mixed, Black 11%)
Per Capita Income: $6,300

Jamaica
Gross Domestic Product: $10,080,000,000 (2002)
Population: 2,695,867
Per Capita Income: $3,800

Brazil
Gross Domestic Product: $1,376,000,000,000
Population: 182, 032, 604 (mixed Black & white 38%, Black 11%)
Per Capita Income: $7,600

Kenya
Gross Domestic Product: $32,890,000,000
Population: 31, 639, 091
Per Capita Income: $1,100

The Company's Wage Structure	Annual PCI	Annual Weeks	1 Weeks Wage	Working Hours Per Week	Hourly Wage	The Company's Basic Wage Scale	The Company's CPI
South Africa	$10,000	52	$192.31	40	$4.81	$6.00	$12,480.00
Black USA	$15,441	52	$296.94	40	$7.42	$10.00	$20,800.00
Haiti	$1,400	52	$26.92	40	$0.67	$3.00	$6,240.00
Nigeria	$900	52	$17.31	40	$0.43	$4.00	$8,320.00
Dominican Republic	$6,300	52	$121.15	40	$3.03	$5.00	$10,400.00
Jamaica	$3,800	52	$73.08	40	$1.83	$4.00	$8,320.00
Brazil	$7,600	52	$146.15	40	$3.65	$6.00	$12,480.00
Kenya	$1,100	52	$21.15	40	$0.53	$3.00	$6,240.00

Strategy For Dealing With Countries With Significant Black Populations Analysis*

*Non-Black populations in these countries have a much higher annual CPI than Blacks. For example; The USA CPI is $36,300 while the Black USA CPI is only $15,441. The Company's strategy will have a far greater impact on Blacks. The $10 per hour minimum wage in the USA does not include benefits. The Company's wage structure in foreign countries includes benefits.

South Africa has an annual (PCI) Per Capita Income of $10,000. As you can see the average hourly rate CPI is $4.81 dollars (US) per hour. The Company's minimum wage will be about $6.00 per hour including benefits. One of South Africa's provinces is called KwaZulu, which means place of the paradise dwellers. I'm afraid it may be necessary for South Africa to restart its nuclear bomb program. There is no doubt this technology is going to spread and Mother Africa must be protected.
New Company CPI = $12,480

The USA has a Black PCI of $15,441. The average hourly CPI is $7.42. The Company's minimum wage will be $10 per hour not including benefits.
The Company's New CPI = $20,800.

Haiti has a CPI of $1,400. The average hourly CPI is 67 cents ($.67) per hour. The Company's minimum wage will be $3.00 per hour including benefits.

The Company's new CPI = $6,240. Many Haitians are now eating dirt.

Nigeria has a CPI of $900. The average hourly CPI is 43 cents ($.43) per hour. The Company's minimum wage will be $4.00 per hour.
Company's New CPI = $8,320.

The Dominican Republic has a CPI of $6,300. The average hourly CPI is $3.03 per hour. The Company's minimum wage will be $5.00 per hour including benefits.
The Company's new CPI = $10,4000.

Jamaica has a CPI of $3,800. The hourly CPI is $1.83. The Company's minimum wage will be $4.00 per hour including benefits.
The Company's new CPI = $8,320.

Brazil's CPI is $7,600. The hourly CPI is $3.65. The Company's minimum wage will be $6.00 including benefits.
The Company's new CPI = $12,480.

Kenya's CPI is $1,100. The hourly CPI is 53 cents ($.53). The Company's minimum wage will be $3.00 per hour including benefits.
The Company's new CPI = $6,240

To an American these foreign wages are low but on must compare that to the world's new economic giant, China. According to Merrill Weingrod of China Strategies factory wages in China's booming east coast cities range from $120 to $160 per month and half that in the country's interior provinces. Average city incomes in Chinese cities are just $1,000 per year, which is 3 times that of the countryside. If you look at what you buy most of it has a "made in China" label on it. $1 an hour in most African countries is a high wage rate. Everything is relative.

Speaking of China, Chinese contact with Africans goes way back. Long ago giant Chinese ships traded with the east coast of Africa. There were Africans living in the great Chinese city (I forgot the name) that was the focal point of the trade. They sailed on baochuans, giant 9 mast ships over 400 feet long. Even today Chinese pottery artifacts can be found in Kenya. The ships the Chinese sailed were 10 times as large as the ships sailed by Columbus.

The Chinese took lions, giraffes, etc. back to China. A power struggle in China destroyed the trade with Africa. It was the merchant traders against the palace eunuchs. The eunuchs saw the trade as a threat to their power. They eventually won and the penalty was death for building large ships. That's the only reason we're not all speaking Chinese today.

K'ung-Fu-Tzu, a famous Chinese philosopher, developed several principles that Black people can learn from, Zhong, Shu and Xiao.

(1) Zhong – doing your best, being conscientious, and being loyal

(2) Shu - Altruism and consideration for others. What you don't want don't do to others

(3) Xiao – Honor one's ancestors

My favorite K'ung saying is "if you want to establish yourself, establish others"

Today we know K'ung-Fu-Tzu as Confucious.

The Question Becomes

The question becomes, why should we pay these people so much money? An American may consider a wage of $3 per hour (including benefits) nothing but to an average Kenyan it's a very high wage. We can get high quality employees at a reasonable price. The question then becomes, what about people in Asia, who are making $1 an hour? They're more educated and therefore more productive also than Kenyans also. Our strategy is not to compete in terms of price only.

If a towel made in Asia costs $3 in a store in New York City then a Kenyan made one may cost $3.25 to account for the lower productivity. However the economic effect on Black people globally will be extremely positive. The fabric company workers in Kenya, shipping companies, distributors, transportation companies, retailers and their employees all benefit from the sales of that 1 towel. Multiply that towel by 5,000,000 annually. That's $16,250,000 per year. If you use an economic multiplier of 7 (I'll get to the economic multiplier) then the total positive effect is $113,500,000. This will create a market for African American businesses as Africans become more prosperous.

Pricing Strategy "The Suits"

The Company's strategy is to play the hand Black people have been dealt. Nature abhors a vacuum and so does economics. There's such a great difference between our spending and our economic development that it's ridiculous. The strategy is to take advantage of our economic differences.

I'll use suits as an example. Let's look at the USA, South Africa and Haiti. The best way to attack a problem is to us the KISS formula. As many of you know KISS means Keep It Simple Stupid. If a suit costs $300.00 in a store in Atlanta it should be made in America. If it costs $200.00 it should be made in South Africa. If it costs $125.00 it should be made in Haiti.

The effect is that people can make a good living in each country making suits. There are several levels of quality in almost everything and we'll use that fact. I'm sure we can secure a strategic alliance with American textile manufacturers. It would even pay to ship American cloth Africa to be made into clothing and then shipped back here for sale. It would raise the cost of some items but the power we would have would make the extra cost insignificant.

The Economic Multiplier, the real reason we're poor

From J.W. Smith's (Economic Democracy: The Political Struggle for the 21ˢᵗ Century), "If a society spends $100 to manufacture a product within its borders, the money that is used to pay for materials, labor and other costs moves through the economy as each resident spends it. Due to the multiplier effect, $100 worth of primary production can add several hundred dollars to the Gross Domestic Product (GDP) of that society. If the money is spent in another society, circulation of that money, and thus the wealth generated, is within that other society"

We are not circulating our money among ourselves. That's the real problem with the way we do things.

===

NOTES

The College Strategy

In order to be truly free we must develop our own systems for enhancing our economic power. Almost every month there's a story in the media about a Black college on the verge of closing. I went to Fordham University, a Catholic university in New York City however as a Black person I'm concerned. The Dance Theater of Harlem and other entities are also in a constant struggle for financing. The Company's solution is to harness the resources we have to eliminate these problems.

The Black colleges can be major players in building wealth in the Black community. They all have large auditoriums, gyms and athletic fields. Let's stop whining about what we don't have and start using what we do have. With that in mind I've developed a strategy for circulating our money among ourselves, benefit Black colleges and strengthen the arts community.

The following pages are my analysis of what can be done.

PLEASE NOTE: The following chart is in thousands,
For example: 5,000 will be 5K

INCOME – College Strategy

Auditorium			Friday	Saturday	Sunday 1	Sunday 2		
	Seats		5,000	5,000	5,000	5,000	Total Concert Goers	6 Weekend Season
Concert Goers								
1- Non-investors			.5K	.5K	.5K	.5K	2K	12K
2-Investors			1K	1K	1K	1K	4K	24K
3- $75 Tickets			1K	1K	1K	1K	4K	24K
4- $100 Tickets			.7K	.7K	.7K	.7K	2.8K	16.8K
5- $125 Tickets			.5K	.5K	.5K	.5K	2K	12K
6- $150 Tickets			.3K	.3K	.3K	.3K	1.2K	7.2K
7- Total Seats Sold			4K	4K	4K	4K	16K	96K
Concert Income								
8- Non Investors			25K	25K	25K	25K	100K	600K
9- Current Investors			50K	50K	50K	50K	200K	1,200K
10- $75 Tickets			75K	75K	75K	75K	300K	1,800K
11- $100 Tickets			70K	70K	70K	70K	280K	1,680K
12- $125 Tickets			62.5K	62.5K	62.5K	62.5K	250K	1,500K
13- $150 Tickets			45K	45K	45K	45K	180K	1,080K
14- Total Concert Income			327.5K	327.5K	327.5K	327.5K	1,310K	7,860K

Expenses – College Strategy

		Friday	Saturday	Sunday 1	Sunday 2	Total Concert Goers	6 Weekend Season
15- Rent		50K	50K	50K	50K	200K	1,200K
16- Donation		10K	10K	10K	10K	40K	240K
17- Scholarships		15K	15K	15K	15K	60K	360K
18- Coupons		60K	60K	60K	60K	240K	1,440K
Established Talent							
19- Diamond		75K	0	0	0	75K	450K
20- Platinum		0	75K	0	0	75K	450K
21- Gold		0	0	75K	0	75K	450K
New Talent							
Silvers							
23	Music	4K	4K	4K	4K	16K	96K
24	Comedy	4K	4K	4K	4K	16K	96K
25	Acrobats	4K	4K	4K	4K	16K	96K

Other Expenses

		Saturday	Friday	Sunday 1	Sunday 2	Total Concert Goers	6 Weekend Season
26- Limos		2K	2K	2K	2K	8K	48K
27- Security		4K	4K	4K	4K	16K	96K
28- Hotel		2K	2K	2K	2K	8K	48K
29- Meals		1K	1K	1K	1K	4K	24K
30- Celebrities		2K	2K	2K	2K	8K	48K

Direct Investment

			Sunday	Saturday	Sunday 1	Sunday 2	Total Concert Goers	6 Weekend Season
$25 Accounts			15K	15K	15K	15K	60K	360K
$50 Accounts			24.5K	24.5K	24.5K	24.5K	98K	588K
$75 Accounts			28.12K	28.12K	28.12K	28.12K	112.5K	675K
$100 Accounts			24K	24K	24IK	24K	96K	576K
Total Direct Investment			91.6K	91.6K	91.6K	91.6K	366.5K	2.199K

Explanation of The College Strategy

This is an illustration of the positive economic effect The Company intends to have on Black economic development using an average Black college as an example.

Total Seats: The College has an auditorium with a total of 5,000 seats. The Company will present shows on Friday night, Saturday evening, a Sunday matinee and finally a Sunday evening show. The basic ticket price is $50. The $50 includes a concert ticket and a $15 coupon redeemable at restaurants, hairdressers, clothing stores or any business associated with The Company or the college. The $15 coupon can be redeemed at any place nationwide that has an investment account with The Company.

Concert Goers: The Company sells 80% of the seats for each concert. 80% 0f 5,000 is 4,000. The 4,00 seats are divided into several categories. 16,000 tickets are sold over the weekend.

Line 1 - Non-investors: These are people who just came to see the concert. They are not investing in The Company's investment fund. They buy 500 $50 tickets per concert.

Line 2– Current Investors: These are The Company's clients who hopefully are bringing friends to the concert. They purchase 1,000 $50 tickets per concert.

Line 3- $75 Tickets: These are new investors who purchase a $50 concert tickets and open a $25 per month investment account with The Company. They purchase 1,000 $75 tickets per show.

Line 4- $100 Tickets: New Investors who purchase a $50 tickets and open a $50 monthly investment account with The Company. They purchase 700 tickets per concert.

Line 5- $125 Tickets: New investors with a $50 ticket and a $75 per month investment account with The Company. The purchase 500 tickets per show.

Line 6 - $150 Tickets: New Investors who receive a $50 ticket and open a $100 per month investment account. They average 300 tickets per concert.

Line 7- Total Tickets Sold: A total of 4,000 tickets per concert are sold. The weekend total is 16,000.

Concert Income

Line 8- Non-investors: $50 times Line 1 = $25,000 per concert. $100,000 for the weekend.

Line 9 – Current Investors: $50 times Line 2 = $50,000 per show. $200,000 for the weekend.

Line 10 - $75 Tickets: $75 times Line 3 = $75,000 per show. $300,000 for the weekend.

Line 11 - $100 Tickets: $100 times Line 4. $280,000 for the weekend.

Line 12 - $125 Tickets: $125 time Line 5 = $62,500 per show. $250,000 for the weekend.

Line 13 - $150 Tickets: $150 times Line 6 = $45,00 per concert. $180,000 for the weekend.

Line 14 – Total Concert Income: All tickets sales combined = $327,500 per concert. $1,310,000 for the weekend.

Expenses – The expenses are designed to popularize the college strategy by providing significant economic activity for the local Black community.

Line 15 – Rent: This is the fee The Company will pay the college for the use of it's facilities per show. In this example a figure of $25,000 per show is used. That means that the school will receive $100,000 for the weekend.

Line 16 – Donation: The Company will give a donation equal to $2 per seat per show to the college. Since there are 5,000 seats and that equals $10,000 per show. The weekend total will be $40,000.

Line 17 – Targeted Scholarships: The Company will give $3 per seat to a targeted scholarship fund. Since there are 5,000 seats in the auditorium that means that $15,000 will be given per concert. That's $60,000 for the weekend. The targeted scholarships will be for students majoring in fields The Company believes is necessary in order to build a global economic empire. Mathematics, physics, chemistry, computer science, engineering and other "hard" disciplines will be supported.

The college has a total income of $200,000 for the weekend. The college can also independently solicit donations from concertgoers. The college can also sell college T-shirts, sweat suits or anything else they want to sell.

Line 18 – Coupons: Each ticket will include a coupon worth $15 at any business associated with The Company. The coupon will also be redeemable at any business globally associated with The Company. For example: a couple buys 2 tickets. 2 tickets mean that they have $30 to use for a dinner, at the hairdresser, at the limo service, etc. The Company will assist colleges in acquiring "strategic partners". A strategic partner could be a quality restaurant in a city near the college. The restaurant will agree because this will lead to an enormous increase in business. It's good for the college because a deal can be made with the restaurant to give a donation to the college for every coupon turned in. In many areas there are not enough Black owned quality restaurants to handle the large number of concertgoers. That means that many white owned restaurants will have to be recruited until we can build more Black owned quality restaurants. Some customers can be served meals at the college cafeteria.

Talent: The Company believes that if the quality of talent at the colleges is high enough the concerts will be successful. The concerts are part of The Company's marketing budget. The Company's goal is to increase the number of investors in its' fund. The Company can only succeed if it creates massive wealth for the Black race. That's the way The Company will be set up. The fact that The Company can assist the Black colleges and Black businesses is just icing on the cake.

Line 19 –Diamond Talent: The Company estimates that Diamond Talent will cost about $50,000 per concert for the weekend.

The Company hopes to include talent that will guarantee a crowd. Stars such as Smokey Robinson, James Brown, Eric Clapton, B.B. King, Lionel Ritchie, Dance Theatre of Harlem and of course Michael. The total major talent budget is estimated to be $200,000 for the weekend.

Line 20 Platinum Talent: These are entertainers on the next level. Since the major talent budget is $50,000 per concert The Company could employ 2 Platinum acts for the price of 1 Diamond act.

Line 21 – Gold Talent: The Company could hire 5 acts at $10,000 per concert using the $50,000 per show budget.

Line 22 - Silvers: Silvers are new acts The Company will be premiering at the concerts.

Line 23 – Silver Musicians: The Company will have about 2 new groups to be warm-up acts for the major talent. $2,000 per act per concert each. The budget in this example is $16,000 for the weekend. The concertgoers will determine which acts progress by their reaction to the performances. The Company will seek out Jazz, Rock, Soul and ethnic music acts. The Company will not feature Rap music because some of it denigrates our people and especially our women. Rappers are just mimicking the white man's tradition of talking trash.

In an article in the New York Daily News on Monday June 7, 2004 Stanley Crouch quotes an 1837 passage from Davy Crockett's Almanac. It is as follows "I can walk like an ox, swim like an eel, run like a fox, yell like an Indian, fight like a devil, spout like an earthquake, make love like a mad bull, and swallow a nigger without choking if you butter his head and pin his ears back". Sounds like the latest hit record.

Speaking of music, I read that Ludwig von Beethoven hung out with a Black composer when he was a young man in Germany. Beethoven got the famous notes for the 5[Th] Symphony from a bird in the Black Forest. Hank Williams, the great Country & Western icon, used to hang out with a Black man when he was a boy. We all know about Elvis. I'll give Elvis credit for making one the most beautiful records about the community ever made. "In The Ghetto" is as beautiful as it is sad.

Line 24 – Silver Comedy: The Company will employ new comedians as part of the war-up portion of the shows. In this example $4,000 is budgeted per show for comedians. The Company could employ 4 new comedians, give them 10 minutes each and let them sink or swim. If the concertgoers like them, they will rise. The Company will reflex the interests of the people.

Line 25 – Silver Acrobats, etc: Various acts that will be entertaining. The budge is $4,000 per show and $16,000 for the weekend.

Line 26 – Limo Services: $2,000 per show for The Company & guests such as entertainers. This will be a good source of income for local limo services. Total over 4 shows is $8,000.

Line 27 – Security: $4,000 per show, $16,000 over the weekend. The Company will contract security firms to handle these duties.

Line 28 – Hotel: $2,000 per show, $8,000 for the weekend for The Company and guest such as entertainers. The Company will utilize local hotels until we can construct our own facilities.

Line 29 – Meals: $1,000 per show for The Company & entertainment, $4,000 for the weekend. The college can recommend local restaurants to The Company.

Line 30 – Celebrities: There are a large number of Black celebrities that Black people will never get to see. For example; The Company will attempt to engage athletes such as Evelyn Ashford, the great sprinter and Tommy "The Hit Man" Hearns to appear as guest greeters to concert goers. The budget is for $1,000 per show each. Their hotel, airfare and limo expenses will also be paid by The Company.

The $10 Bucket of Chicken

Black people love fried chicken.
The following example illustrates how something as simple as buying a bucket of chicken can create great wealth. Fried chicken is producing great wealth now but not for us. The $10 bucket of chicken you buy is just the final financial transaction in a long chain of transactions, none of which involves you.

That reminds me of what one of my best friends told me about a butcher in upper Manhattan. It seems that his sister was head cook for a Head Start program that fed over 100 children per day. Every week she went to this butcher and ordered over $700 in meat, thousands of dollars per month. Then one day while she was in the butcher shop she remembered that there was a fundraiser for the Head Start program. She asked the butcher if he could make a small donation, say $10. He told her that he doesn't make donations and refused to give her anything. That's the attitude we're dealing with. A can't imagine even a white butcher refusing to give $25 dollars. So much for people of color.

We have to do what other people do. If we like Chinese or any other type of food we should deal with our friends, spouses families only. That's what Jews do and we have to do the same. If industry that Jews are strong in they promote their children, wives and girlfriends. There's nothing wrong with, we just need to do it too.

When you break up a price into its components that lead to it things become obvious. The example is a conservative guess of how much a chicken place can earn in the Black community.

PLEASE NOTE: BECAUSE OF THE SIZE AND VAST AMOUNT OF NUMBERS INCLUDED IN THE FINANCIAL CHARTS OF THIS BOOK MANY NUMBERS WILL BE IN THE THOUSANDS. FOR EXAMPLE: $400,000 WILL BE $400K.

Bucket of Chicken Chart

	1 Bucket	200 Buckets Daily	Monthly Sales	1 Year Chicken Place	50 Chicken Places	Average Salary	Jobs Created	Econ. Mult.	Total Jobs Created
Price	$10	$2K	$60K	$720K	36,000K				
Expenses									
	Unit Costs								
Lawyer	$.20	$40	$1.2K	$14.4K	$720K	$50K	15	8	120
Acct.	$.15	$30	.9K	$10.8K	$540K	$35K	15	8	120
Printing	$.05	$10	.3K	$3.6K	$180K	20K	9	8	72
Delivery 1	$.20	$40	$1.2K	$14.4K	$720K	$30K	24	8	192
Delivery 2	$.20	$40	$1.2K	$14.4K	$720K	$30K	24	8	192
Delivery 3	$.20	$40	$1.2K	$14.4K	$720K	$30K	24	8	192
Pest Control	$.05	$10	.3K	$3.6K	$180K	$35K	5	8	40
Light/Heat	$.50	$100	$3K	$36K	$1,800K	$50K	36	8	288
Air Cond.	$.50	$100	$3K	$36K	$1,800K	$50K	36	8	288
Chicken Wholesaler	$2.00	$400	$12K	$144K	$7,200K	$30K	240	8	1,920
Staff	$2.00	$400	$12K	$144K	$7,200K	$25K	288	8	2,304
Beverages	$.50	$100	$3K	$36K	$1,800K	$25K	72	8	576
Rent			$6K	$72K	$3,600K	$72K	50	8	400
Total Expenses	$6.55	$1,310	$45.3K	$543.6K	$27,180K		838	8	6,704
Profit	$3.45	$690	$14.7K	$176.4K					

Bucket of Chicken Chart Bucket of Chicken explanation

The price of 1 bucket of chicken is of course $10.00. If you divide all the costs of delivering the bucket of chicken to you it becomes obvious that something this simple is creating millionaires. For this example I've estimated the expenses and profits associated with that $10 bucket of chicken. As you can see many businesses get a piece of the pie. In this case the expenses total $6.55 per bucket of chicken. Lawyers, accountant, truck drivers, etc. all benefit from this bucket of chicken. None of your neighbors get a cent. There are no jobs for your son who is unemployed. There is not one administrative assistant position at the lawyer's office for your daughter trying to get on her feet.

The profit in this case is $3.45 per bucket. If 200 buckets of chicken sold in a day then that's $690 per in profits.

If you multiply the $690 by per day by 30 days the monthly profit is $14,700.

$14,700 per month in profits times 12 months is $176,400.00 per year. How many Black people you know who makes $176,400 per year.

In many Black areas there are numerous chicken places. Let's take Queens New York as an example. I didn't go around and count the chicken places but I'm sure there are more than 50 in Black communities in Queens. I'll use 50 as an example.

If 1 store has a profit of $176,400 per year then 50 stores profit is $8,820,000. Numbers don't lie.

Look at the average salaries' estimate and the 838 jobs directly created.

The economic multiplier increases the wealth of communities by circulating dollars among the local people. I've used a moderate multiplier of 8. Multipliers can be much higher than this. The multiplier has nothing do with Black people because we are not in the income stream we just supply the seed money. In this example the result is 6,704 jobs being supported just in Queens by us just buying chicken. This is very low estimate.

This example applies to everything we buy not just chicken.

e must take over business in our community if our youth are to have a future.

The Players*

In order to make the potential benefits of cooperating more real I created *The Players*. *The Players* are a representative sample of individuals found in the African American community. The Company expects non-Blacks to invest also. We will follow *The Players* through the financial charts and observe how each person benefits in their own way. This book was intended to be in color, however in order to lower the cost to the consumer the book is in black and white. Special Edition color versions will soon become available.

The Players are:

1 - Computer Expert, code color= Blue

He knows all the latest computer software and hardware. He is especially strong in graphics, desktop publishing, etc. His dream of starting his own computer school is just that, a dream.

2 - Small Construction Company Owner, code color= Red

This company is making it but they're not making it big. They get contracts but not that big and not that many. They perform quality work. They treat their customers with respect.

3 - Welfare Mother (2 kids), code color = Orange

She has made serious errors in judgment. The fathers of her 2 children are not worthy of the title "Father". They're not supporting their children financially or morally. She is however very tough. She's determined to make something of her life. Fashion is her passion.

4– Married Bus Driver and Secretary, code color = Yellow

This couple has a deep sincere pride in being Black and they instill that pride in their children. Their children realize it's important to know the great people in African American history. They also realize that their children should know Shakespeare, Einstein, and Thomas Jefferson. They are looking toward the future. They like the idea of making a living with an import/export business.

5- Street Corner Brother, code color = Gold

A loser. He's like a lot of brothers who don't have a chance. He's held down not by white people but by Blacks. He was unfortunate enough to appear as a pure African to other African Americans. His skin is dark and that makes him a nobody.

He can out curse anybody on the corner. He can find a gun if he has to. He is loud and dresses like he's homeless. He paid over $400 for the clothes he's wearing but he looks like he's homeless to a normal person. He realizes life is passing him by and is seeking a change. He likes to cook and stares at restaurants.

6- Grandmother (2 grandchildren, ages 6 and 10), code color = Pink

She's in her sixties and just loves her grandkids, 1 boy and 1 girl. She wants them to be successful when they grow up. That's all there is.

7 – Non-Black Architect living in the suburbs, code color = Brown
He like the Blacks involved is looking to make a buck

8 - Truck Driver, color code = Purple
He drives for UPS, or FedEx, etc. He knows a nice young lady that is the one for him. He wants to be a man and provide for her. He is a very good driver.

9 – Janitor, code color = Silver
He likes his work. He correctly believes that any honest work is honorable. Some of his friends chose to lose. They got involved in crime and are in and out of jail. He'd rather be a janitor. He is also good at maintenance.

10 – Lawyer, color code = Green, the color of money
He's making a decent living but something's missing. He wants to feel that he's making a positive contribution. He wonders how can he do this and live good also.

PLEASE NOTE: A BLACK BACKGROND INDICATE MORE THAN 1 Player
INVOLVED.

==

The following Exhibits and Schedules are from the master plan

Exhibit A

Investors By Selected Months in Year 1

Cumulative

	Investors	*Players*	Month	1	4	8	12		Year
Line 3 Cum.	$25 Accounts	O.G.S.		1,000	18,000	143,000	593,000		593,000
Line 6 Cum.	$50 Accounts	Y, P		500	7,375	68,313	376,809		376,809
Line 9 Cum.	$100 Accounts	Pu		250	4,250	22,268	66,256		66,256
Line 12 Cum.	$200 Accounts	Br		50	765	3,636	8,658		8,658

Line 15 Cum.	$300 Accounts			25	1,630	9,268	20,499		20,499
Line 18 Cum.	$400 Accounts			10	1,041	5,566	11,067		1,067
Line 21 Cum.	$500 Accounts	Bl		5	519	2,782	5,535		5,533
Line 24 Cum.	$1,000 Accounts	Gr, R		2	110	563	1,113		1,113
Line 25 Cum.	Total Monthly Investors			1,842	33,690	255,396	1,082,937		1,082,937

Exhibit A – Investor Totals by Month

Explanation of Exhibit A

Exhibit A is an estimate of the number of investors by month for the 1st year. The numbers at the left of the account amounts is a line reference number. The accounts are categorized by the amount of investment per investor per month. There are $25, $50, $100, $200, $300, $400, $500 and $1,000 monthly accounts in this example. The number of investors will increase gradually as time goes by. The reason the investment accounts start as low as $25 is because we want everyone in the community regardless of their income to get involved. If the accounts start at $100 for instance, the Black masses will not invest in it and they must participate for this to work. The New Investors line shows the number of new investors coming into the plan each month. The Active Accounts are investors who are investing in accounts they've begun earlier. The Cumulative (Cum.) Accounts are New Investors plus Active Investors. Look at:

The Players

Line 1-New $25 Accounts.
There were 1,000 $25 investors in the first month (Month). Included in those 1,000 investors were 3 Players; The Welfare Mother, The Street Corner Brother and The Janitor. In Month 2 there are 2,000 new investors at $25 per month each. When you add the investors from Month 1 the total number of $25 investors is 3,000. This formula applies to every monthly total.

The Computer expert (Blue) invests $500 per month, Line 19

The Small Construction Company (Red) invests $1,000 per month, Line 22

The Welfare Mother (Orange) invests $25 per month, Line 1

The married couple, The Bus Driver & The Secretary (Yellow) invest $50 per month together, Line 4

The Street Corner Brother (Gold) invests $25 per month, Line 1

The Grandmother (Pink) invests $50 per month in the names of her 2 grandchildren. They are ages 6 and 10. Line 4

The Non-Black Architect (Brown) invests $200 per month, Line 10

The Truck Driver (Purple) invests $100 per month, Line 7

The Janitor (Silver) invests $25 per month, Line 1

The Lawyer (Green) invests $1,000 per month, Line 22

==

NOTES

Exhibit B
Investment By Selected Months
(In Thousands)

Month		*Players*	1	4	8	12		Year 1 Total
Line 1								
$25 Accounts		O,G,S	$25K	$450K	$3,575K	$14,825K		$48,225K
Line 2								
$50 Accounts		Y,P	$25K	$368K	$3,415K	$18,840K		$52,940K
Line 3								
$100 Accounts		Pu	$25K	$425K	$2,226K	$6,625K		$25,102K
Line 4								
$200 Accounts		Br	10K	$153K	$727K	$1,426K		$7,439K
Line 5								
$300 Accounts			$7.5K	$489K	$2,786K	$6,149K		$27,138K
Line 6								
$400 Accounts			$4K	$416K	$2,226K	$4,428K		$20,800K
Line 7								
$500 Accounts		Bl	$2.5K	$259K	$1,391K	$2,766K		$12,994K
Line 8								
$1,000 Accounts		Gr, R	$2K	$110K	$562K	$1,112K		$5,265K
Line 9								
Total Gross Investment			$101K	$2,671K	$16,911K	$56,478K		$199,906K

74

Explanation of Exhibit B – Gross Investment, First Year

Exhibit B is the total amount of investment received in each account category. For instance look at the $25 Accounts. The Exhibit A Table shows that 1,000 investors (Line 1) invested $25 in the 1ˢᵗ month. Exhibit B says that those 1,000 investors invested $25,000, which is 1,000 times $25 (Line 1). On Exhibit A there are only 2 investors who invest $1,000 the first month (Line 8), therefore the total investment for the $1,000 Accounts is $2,000. The investment total does not reflex fees taken by The Company to manage the accounts.

The Players

The Welfare Mother (Orange)
Street Corner Brother Gold
Janitor (Silver)
each invests $25 dollars each per month. Line 1

The married couple (Bus Driver & Secretary, Yellow) investments $50 per month, Line 2

The Grandmother (Pink) invests $50 per month, Line 2

The Truck Driver (Purple) invests $100 per month, Line 3

The Non-Black architect (Brown) invests $200 per month, Line 4

The Computer Expert (Blue) invests $500 per month, Line 7

The Small Construction (Red) invests $1,000 per month, Line 8

The Lawyer (Green) invests $1,000 per month, Line 8

===

NOTES

Exhibit C – Net Investment

(In thousands)

Month	Players	1	4	8	12	Year 1 Total
1 - $25 Accounts	O,G,S	$15K	$270K	$2,145K	$8,695K	$28,935K
2- $50 Accounts	Y,P	$17.5K	$258K	$2,390K	$13,188K	$37,058K
3- $100 Accounts	PU	$21.25K	$361.25K	$1,892K	$5,631K	$21,337K
4- $200 Accounts	Br	$9K	$137.7K	$654K	$1,558K	$6,695K
5- $300 Accounts		$6,75K	$440K	$2,507K	$5,534K	$24,424K
6- $400 Accounts		$3.6K	$374.6K	$2,003K	$3,984K	$18,720K
7- $500 Accounts	Bl	$2.25K	$233.7K	$1,251K	$2,489K	$11,695K
8- $1,000 Accounts	Gr, R	$1.9K	$104.6K	$534K	$1,057K	$5,002K
9- The Company's Investment		0	0	$250K	$250K	$1,250K
10- Total Investment		$77.25K	$2,180K	$13,631K	$85,178K	$155,118K
11- Direct Investment		$154.5K	$4,360K	$27,262		$310,236K

Explanation of Exhibit C

Exhibit C is the Net Investment Table. The Net Investment equals the Gross Investment (Exhibit B) minus The Company's fees. The Company will use these fees to set up offices, hire staff, advertise, customer service, etc. The amount of the fee depends on the size of the investment. The fee rates range from 40% for $25 Accounts to 10% for Accounts of $200 or more monthly. The reason the small investment has a larger fee rate is because it has to be serviced just like much larger accounts. All The Company's employees will be investors also. The Company will treat all investors the same. Of course if one investor is needed before another one they will be contacted first. For instance, lawyers, construction companies and architects will be utilized early.

The reason is that we will be building and upgrading stores, strip malls, etc. and most of these projects will require lawyers, construction companies and architects. Some of the other investors will own these businesses after the architects, construction companies, accountants, etc. have set them up.
For example on Exhibit C the monthly fee rates are as follows:
$25 Accounts – 40% per month
$50 Accounts – 30% per month
$100 Accounts – 15% per month
$200 Accounts – 10% per month
$300 Accounts – 10% per month
$400 Accounts – 10% per month
$500 Accounts – 10% per month
$1,000 Accounts – 5% per month

On Exhibit B (Gross Investment) the total of $25 Accounts is $25,000 (Line 1). After deducting The Company's fees the Net Investment (Exhibit C) is $15,000 (Line 1). $15,000 is 60% of $25,000. The other 40% is The Company's fee. Why such a high fee for very small accounts? The Company will have to service this investor as if they had a big account. As the investment amount increases The Company's fees decrease as a percentage of the investment. Many of these small investors eventually will be working for The Company as Customer Service Agents. Many more will get business loans.

Another example; On Exhibit B the total investment for $1,000 accounts is $2,000 (Line 8). Here on Exhibit C the Net Investment is $1,900. $1,900 is 95% of $2,000. The Company's fee is $100 (5%).

The Players

The Welfare Mother, The Street Corner Brother and The Janitor each have a $25 per month account. Line 1

The married couple, the Bus Driver and the Secretary, (Yellow) and The Grandmother (Pink) have $50 accounts. Line 2

The Truck Driver (Purple), has a $100 per month account, Line 3

Non-Black Architect (Brown) has a $200 per month account, Line 4

The Computer Expert (Blue) has a $500 per month account, Line 7

The Lawyer (Green) and the Small Construction Company (Red) have $1,000 accounts, Line 8

The Company will invest it's own funds also. The Company will usually be the largest investor. We will not want to be left out. Line 9

Total Net Investment, Line 10

Direct Loans – Since The Company will be a financial institution it will be able lend at least twice the monthly Net investment. Line 11

===

NOTES

Schedule 1 – Base Businesses Financed
Distributors, Manufacturers, Wholesalers & Import/ Export

Explanation of Schedule 1

Schedule 1

Businesses Financed Distributors/Wholesalers/Importers	Month 1	4	8	12	Year 1
1-Furniture ($200,000 each) S	0	0	2	3	15
2-Home Appliances ($250,000 each) R	0	0	2	3	15
3-Women/Girls Clothing ($150,000 each) Y	0	0	2	3	15
4-Men/Boys Clothing ($150,000 each) Y	0	1	2	3	16
5-Hardware ($100,000 each)	0	1	2	3	16
6-Electronics ($150,000 each) Br	0	1	2	3	16
7-Auto Products $200,000 each) Bl	0	1	2	3	16
8-Food except meat ($250,000 each) Gr	0	1	2	3	17
9-Meat/Fish/Poultry ($200,000 each) Gr	0	1	2	3	17
10-Beer & Ale ($100,000 each) Pu	0	1	2	3	16
11-Restaurant Equipment ($250,000 each), R	0	1	2	3	17
12-Distilled Spirits & Wine ($150,000 each) R	0	1	2	3	16
13-Jewelry (($100,000 each)	0	1	2	3	16
14-Sporting Goods ($100,000 each) Gr	0	0	2	3	15
15-Shoes ($75,000 each)	0	0	2	3	15
16-Miscellaneous Projects ($100,000 each) Pu	0	0	2	3	15
17- Total Dist./Wholes/Importers	0	10	32	48	253

Base businesses are businesses that will feed the retail businesses inventory and services. Often when Blacks try to start a business they are held back because they don't know how to obtain inventory or supplies and if they do they're overcharged. In one case a Black business was told that if they carry Louis Farrakhan's product line his own products would be boycotted by distributors. We have to have our own network of companies that we control so we can be free.

Next to each broad business category is an estimate of how much the business will cost to start. For example, Furniture is the 1st category on Schedule 1. $200,000 is a reasonable amount to set up such a company. The $200,000 will include funds for inventory, setting up a warehouse, legal, etc. It will also include enough cash to operate for several months even if there's no income.

This is called *Working Capital*. The Furniture distributor will supply furniture to other retail furniture store that we will finance. All the businesses on Schedule 1 are designed to supply other businesses. Note that over time the businesses financed increases gradually.

The Company will begin by financing Base Businesses. These are suppliers such as manufacturers, importers, distributors and wholesalers. In our example a Food distributor (except meat), a Meat/Poultry Distributor and a Restaurant Equipment company are financed first.

The Players

During the 1ˢᵗ year the Janitor (Silver) gets a contract to maintain a furniture store, Line 1

The Small Construction Company (Red) receives a contract to work on the Home Appliance Distributor location, Line 2

The married couple (Yellow) receives funding to start a company that will import women/girls and men/boys clothing from Black American designers & Africa (Lines 3 and 4). Africa manufactures some of the best clothing in the world. The Company will send Black designers from the USA to Africa and other countries to design clothing. The Company will also establish a Black fashion industry in the USA in a southern city to be named later. Only by doing this will we be able to prosper from our clothing purchases and this will give our won designers a chance.

The non-Black architect designs an electronics distributor facility, Line 6

The Computer Expert (Blue) sets up an inventor control system for the auto parts distributor, Line 7

The Lawyer (Green) performs legal work for the Food/except meat distributor and the Meat/Fish wholesaler, Lines 8 and 9

The Beer and Ales Distributor has inventory shipped to customer by The Truck Driver's (Purple) company, Line 10

The Small Construction Company (Red) receives contracts from a restaurant equipment distributor and a distilled wine and spirits distributor to upgrade or construct their facility. Lines 11 and 12 .

The Sporting Goods Wholesaler hires the Lawyer (Green) to handle some legal work, Line 14

The Truck Driver (Purple) delivers goods to projects that will come up in the future, Line 16

==

NOTES

Explanation of The Company's Loan Procedures

The Company will finance businesses based upon the Total Person Principle. The Total Person Principle is based upon a 100-point system. The 100 points will be divided into several categories. As of now they are:

1-Character   51%

2-Knowledge   15 %

3-Experience   20%

4-Attitude   10%

5-Charm   4%

The percentages may change as experience dictates

1 – Character: As you clearly can see The Company values a person's character above all. The percentages in the 100 Point System may change. The Company is not interested in owning your home, car, etc. The Company wants you to succeed. Simply filling out the application will test a loan applicant's character. If a person has a criminal record it must be stated on the application. If it is omitted and The Company finds out then that applicant will go to the back of the line of applicants for loans. If however the applicant admits to his criminal record on the application then The Company will consider the application a new beginning for the applicant.

The past will no longer be held against him or her. We want our members to use family and friends for references. The family and friends would be very interested in why you need references. The references will have to accompany the client to The Company's office. Once they find out why you need them they'll be new investors for The Company.

We would expect the applicant not to engage in any more criminal or disrespectful behavior. No robbing, cursing in public, being loud, littering and other negative behavior. The Company cannot enforce these standards but we will encourage positive behavior.

2- Knowledge: In many cases knowledge is more important then anything else. In some fields it's almost as important as character.

3- Experience: Lots of times you'll meet a person who may not be as formally educated as someone else but they know how to do things. This is very true in certain fields such as cooking, truck driving, carpentry, etc.

4-Attitude: If a person is not sincere in their willingness to work to achieve success it will become known. It's your sincere; it's OK to have stars in your eyes.

5- Charm: For certain jobs charm is the key. Some people have personalities that will lead to success because people like them. This is why Oprah Winfrey is a billionaire.

I'll use a typical project the Company will finance using the Players as participants.

In this case the married couple (Yellow) will be used to demonstrate. The couple receives $300K to open an import company specializing in clothing.

Financial Procedures Table

Players	Are	The	Married	Couple		Import/	Export	Co.
	Month	1	2	3	4	5	6	Total
The Company	1- Investment	$25K	25K	25K	$50K	$100K	$75K	$300K
Small Construction Co., R	2-Leasehold Improvement	$0	$0	$0	$10K	$20K	$20K	$50K
Street Corner Brother, G	3- Laborer for Constr. Co.	$0	$0	$0	$2K	$2K	$2K	$6K
Lawyer, Gr	4- Legal	$4K	$2K	$2K	$2K	$2K	$2K	$14K
Other Investor	5-Office Equip.	$0	$0	$0	$0	$20K	$0	$20K
Other Investor	6-Inventory	$0	$0	$0	$0	$15K	$20K	$35
Salaries								
	7-Husband	$0	$0	$0	$4K	$4K	$4K	$12K
	8- Wife	$0	$0	$0	$4K	$4K	$4K	$12K
Other Inv.	9- Advertising	$0	$0	$0	$0	$0	$$15K	$15K
Other Inv.	10- Acct.	$1K	$1K	$1K	$1K	$2K	$2K	$8K
Other Inv.	11- Travel	$0	$0	$2K	$2K	$2K	$3K	$9K
Other Inv.	12- Lodging	$0	$0	$2K	$2K	$2K	$3K	$9K
Computer Expert, Bl	13- Acct. System	$0	$0	$1K	$1K	$1K	$1K	$4K
Welfare Mother, O	14 – Office Asst.	$0	$0	$0	$0	$0	$2K	$2K
Janitor, S	15- Cleaning Contract	$0	$0	$0	$0	$0	$0	$0
Non-Black Investor, Br	16- Architect	$0	$10K	$0	$0	$0	$0	$10K
Truck Driver, Pu	17-Deliveries	$0	$0	$0	$0	$0	$0	$0
Total Funds Used	18	$5K	$13K	$8K	$28K	$74K	$78K	$206K

Cash Balance Monthly	19	$20K	$12K	$17K	$22K	$26k	-3K	$94K
Net Cash Balance	20	$20K	$32K	$49K	$71K	$97K	$94K	

Financial Procedures

The Company will not disburse the total loan amount to a borrower upon approval by The Company's loan committee. To illustrate The Company's method The Married Couple will be used as an example. Remember they're interested in import/export. Suppose The Company chose to finance their business

Please note: In this example "Other Investor" means investors not used in The Players

Line 1- Investment: The Company will set aside the total loan amount but will disburse the funds over a period of months. In this case the loan is for $300,000. The couple will import and purchase domestic clothing for women/girls and men/boys. Since the women/girls and the men/boys clothing distributorships each cost $150,000, the total loan will be for $300,000. They receive $25,000 per month in months 1, 2 and 3. In month 4 they receive $50,000, in month 5 $100,000 and $75,000 in month 6 for a grand total of $300,000.

The Players

Line 2 – Small Construction Co. (R) (Leasehold Improvement): When you organize your business location you will have to customize, repair or improve the location in some form. These are Leasehold Improvements. $10,000 in month 4 and $20,000 in months 5 and 6.

Line 3- Street Corner Brother (G) gets a job as a laborer for The Small Construction Company at $500 per week beginning in month 4.

Line 4 – Lawyer (Gr), Legal Matters: The Company has to be organized properly and a lawyer must be on retainer. $4,000 in month 1, and $2,000 per month in months 2 to 6.

Line 5 – Other Investor, Office Equipment: $20,000 in month 5. Computers, copier, desks, pens, pencils, phone system, chairs, tables, etc.

Line 6 – Other Investor, Inventory: In this case it's merchandise such as dresses, suits, shirts, coats etc. to be sold to retailers. $15,000 in month 5 and $20,000 in month 6.

Salaries – The Company will put every loan recipient on a base salary until the business stabilizes. This will minimize reckless spending.

Line 7- Husband's salary, $1,000 per week, beginning in month 4

Line 8- Wife's salary, $1,000 per week, beginning in month 4

Line 9- Other Investor, Advertising: $15,000 near grand opening (month 6)

Line 10 – Other Investor, Accounting: Bad or inaccurate books can kill a business. Estimate, $1,000 per month in months 1 to 4. $2,000 per month in months 5 and 6.

11 – Other Investor, Travel: As buyers the business owners will have to visit manufacturers. $2,000 per month in months 3 to 5. $3,000 in month 6.

12 – Other Investor, Lodging: same as Travel Expenses per month.

13- Computer Expert (Bl): In most cases the loan recipients will be required to take basic courses on managing their business. Computerized accounting, economics, and business specific courses will constitute the majority of classes. In our example the Married Couple will take courses on the import/export business. $1,000 per month beginning in month 3.

14 – Welfare Mother (O): Gets a job at the Import/Export company at $500 per week in month 6

15- Janitor (S): Janitor secures a contract to clean the office and storage area of the Import/Export Company after grand opening in month 7.

16 – Non-Black architect (Br): $10,000 in month 2 for designing the facility

17-Truck Driver (Pu): Secures contract to deliver merchandise to retailers after grand opening in month 7

18- Total funds used equals all the expenses for that particular month.

19- Cash Balance Monthly: The months' Investment (line 1) minus (-) Total Funds Used (Line 18). In month 1 there's $25,000 in Investment (loan) and $5,000 in expenses. The balance is $20,000. In month 5 there's $100,000 investment and there is $74,000 in expenses. The positive Cash Balance for month 5 is $26,000.

20- Net Ending Cash Balance: The Cash Balance-monthly (Line 20) + the previous months Cash Balance-monthly (Line 19). In month 1 the Net Ending Cash Bank Balance Line 20 is the same ($12,000) as the Cash Balance-monthly (Line 19) because there's no previous month's balance to add. In month 2 the Net Ending Cash Bank Balance (Line 20) is $12,000. That's equal to the Cash Balance-monthly (Line 19) + Net Ending Cash Bank Balance (line 20) for month 1. This is how much money is in the bank at the end of the month.

At the Grand Opening there's $94,000 in the bank

Schedule 2

Investment By Month

Month	1	4	8	12	Total Year 1
Direct Business Loans	$154K	$4,360K	$27,262K	$85,178K	$310,236K
Distributors /Wholesalers /Importers					
1-Furniture ($200K) S	$0	$0	$400K	$600K	$3,000K
2-Home Appliances ($250K) R	$0	$0	$500K	$750K	$3,750K
3-Women/Girls Clothing ($150K) Y	$0	$0	$300K	$450K	$2,250K
4-Men/Boys Clothing ($150K) Y	$0	$150K	$300K	$450K	$2,400K
5-Hardware ($100K)	$0	$100K	$200K	$300K	$1,600K
6-Electronics ($150,000) Br	$0	$150K	$300K	$450K	$2,400K
7-Auto Products $200K) Bl	$0	$200K	$400K	$600K	$3,200K
8-Food except meat ($250K) Gr	$0	$250K	$500K	$750K	$4,250K
9-Meat/Fish/Poultry ($200K) Gr	$0	$200K	$400K	$600K	$3,400K
10-Beer & Ale ($100K) Pu	$0	$100K	$200K	$300K	$1,600K
11-Restaurant Equipment ($250K), R	$0	$250K	$500K	$750K	$4,250K

12-Distilled Spirits & Wine ($150K) R	$0	$150K	$300K	$450K	$2,400K
13-Jewelry ($100K)	$0	$100K	$200K	$300K	$1,600K
14-Sporting Goods ($100K) Gr	$0	$0	$200K	$300K	$1,500K
15-Shoes ($75K)	$0	$0	$150K	$225K	$1,125K
16-Miscellaneous Projects ($100K) Pu, Bl	$0	$0	$200K	$0	$1,000K
17- Total Dist. Wholes/Importers	$0	$1,650K	$5,050K	$7,275K	$39,725K

93

Explanation Of Schedule 2

In our example Schedule 2 shows the cost of financing the Base Businesses. Next to each category is The Company's estimate of the unit cost to start up these companies. The Company estimates that it will cost $250,000 to start a food distributor (except meat), $200,000 for a Meat/Fish Company and $250,000 for a Restaurant Equipment company.

The Players

The Janitor (silver) gets a contract in Month 5 to nightly clean a furniture store, Line 1

As stated in the Financial Procedures The Married Couple (Yellow) is selected by The Company to start an import fashion company. The Company will assist other investors who want to be fashion designers supply inventory to the fashion company. The Company will encourage trade between Africa and the fashion company. In this example The Company begins to finance the business in the 4th month. The total investment will be $300,000 spread over several months. The unit cost of the women/girls and the men/boys importing infrastructures are $150,000 each. See Lines 3 and 4, month 4. The married couple will be used to illustrate how The Company will build Black businesses. As I stated before the total cost of financing the import company is $300,000 (lines 3 and 4). The Company will not give the loans recipients the total amount once the loan has been approved by its loan committee. The Company will employ checks and balances to ensure that these companies have the best chance to succeed. Remember other investors besides The Players are receiving funding that accounts for all the other numbers on the chart.

The non-Black Architect (Brown) gets a contract to design an Electronics Store, Line 6.

The Company assigns the Lawyer (Green) to assist the Food Distributor, except meat, distributor (line 8) and the Meat/Fish/Poultry company (line 9) and the Sporting Goods Company (line 14). Other lawyers who are investors will handle the other companies. The lawyer will be given more clients as we finance more businesses.

The Computer Expert (Blue) is assigned by The Company to set up an accounting, and inventory system for the Auto Parts Distributor, line 7. Later The Company finances the Computer Expert's own computer training school (see Miscellaneous Projects, line 16).

The Small Construction Company (Red) is assigned by The Company to upgrade the buildings that will house the Home Appliance store (line 2), the Restaurant Equipment Company (line 11), and the Distilled Spirits facility (line 12). Contracts awarded by The Company will force The Small Construction Company to hire more and more employees as time goes by. This is the goal of The Company.

During the year The Company finances the Truck Driver's (Purple) own transportation firm, line 16. He also has a contract with a Beer/Ale Company to deliver their products, line 10. His firm will have instant clients since The Company will be financing stores that need his company's services.

The Grandmother's (Pink) grandchildren are too young to run a business. What we will do is start preparing them to be the business leaders of the future. The Company will set up visits to businesses, offer classes, provide academic tutoring etc. to assist them. When they are old enough to get working papers The Company will assist them with summer internships. Classes in etiquette will also be offered. They must become totally confident, respectful and knowledgeable.

===

NOTES

Please Note: Because the charts are so large several months are skipped in the financial charts.

Schedule 3	Month	1	4	8	12	Year 1
Retail Businesses Financed						
1-Small Grocery Stores ($75,000 each) Bl		0	10	25	100	350
2-Medium Grocery Stores ($150,000 each) R		0	2	20	60	212
3-Large Grocery Stores ($500,000 each) S		0	1	10	25	99
4-Women's Clothing ($75,000 each), O		0	1	10	30	102
5-Men's Clothing ($75,000 each) O		0	1	10	30	102
6-Shoes ($35,000 each) O		0	1	10	30	98
7-Travel Agencies ($20,000 each)		0	1	5	20	66
8-Furniture ($75,000 each) Pu		0	1	7	30	97
9-Small Deli ($50,000 each)		0	1	10	30	116
10-Sporting Goods ($75,000 each) R		0	1	8	30	101
11-Restaurant ($200,000 each), G		0	1	7	30	99
12-Laundermat ($75,000 each) R		0	1	8	30	114
13-Optical Goods ($75,000 each) Pu		0	1	6	30	97
14-Auto Parts ($100,000 each) Pu		0	1	10	30	115
15-Dry Cleaners ($75,000 each) G		0	1	8	30	101
16-Mail Box Service ($35,000 each)		0	1	10	30	113
17-Jewelry ($100,000 each) Br		0	0	5	30	84
18-Home Electronics ($75,000 each) S		0	1	10	30	112
19-Meat/Fish/Poultry ($75,000 each)		0	1	10	30	112
20-Hardware ($50,000 each)		0	1	5	20	67
21-Fruits/Vegetables ($50,000 each)		0	1	6	25	86
22-Other Retail ($50,000 each) R		0	1	15	30	149
23-Professional's Offices ($150,000 each) Br		0	2	10	30	116
24-Total Retail Businesses		0	33	225	760	2,708
25-Total New Businesses		0	43	257	808	2,961

Explanation of Schedule 3

Schedule is the ultimate goal of The Company. These are the kinds of businesses that people must use every day. This is where we spend our money and create trillions of dollars in economic benefit for others, but not for ourselves. Food, clothing, lottery games, restaurants, etc. are our targets. Next to each category is The Company's estimate of the cost of each.

The "Total New Businesses" = Schedule 1, Total Dist/Wholesalers/Importers, line 17 + Schedule 3, Total Retail Businesses (line 24)

The Players

The Computer Expert (blue) gets several contracts installing inventory and management systems for Small Grocery Stores, line 1.

The Small Construction Company (Red) is constantly getting bigger, hiring more workers and making more money. The Small Construction Company has contracts to build Medium Grocery Stores (line 2), Sporting Goods Stores, (line 10), Laundromats, (line 12), and Other Retail Businesses, (line 22).

The Janitor (silver) has contracts to clean several Large Grocery Stores, line 3 and a few Home Electronic Stores, line 18.

The Welfare Mother (Orange) gets a loan near the end of the first year to open a store selling Women's and Men's clothing and shoes, lines 4, 5, & 6.

The Truck Driver (purple) gets contracts delivering furniture, line 8, optical goods, line 13 and auto parts, line 14

The Street Corner Brother (gold) has 2 jobs. He started out working for the Small Construction Company, then he began washing dishes at a Restaurant (line 11), and working at a Dry Cleaners also (line 15). He's saving money to open his own deli.

In a few months he has moved up to chef's assistant at the Restaurant. He's on his way.

Non-Black Architect (Brown) gets contracts to design a Jewelry Store, line 17 and a he gets a loan to open a better office, line 23.

==

NOTES

Schedule 4

Retail Outlets	Unit Costs					
Month		1	4	8	12	Year 1
1-Small Grocery Stores ($75K) Bl		$75K	$0	$750K	$1,875K	$7,500K	$26,250K
2-Medium Grocery Stores ($150K) R		$150K	$0	$300K	$3,000K	$9,000K	$31,800K
3-Large Grocery Stores ($500K) S		$500K	$0	$500K	$5,000K	$12,500K	$49,500K
4-Women's Clothing ($75K), O		$75K	$0	$75K	$750K	$2,250K	$7,650K
5-Men's Clothing ($75K) O		$75K	$0	$75K	$750K	$2,250K	$7,650K
6-Shoes ($35K) O		$35K	$0	$35K	$350K	$1,050K	$3,430K
7-Travel Agencies ($20K)		$20K	$0	$20K	$100K	$400K	$1,320K
8-Furniture ($75K) Pu		$75K	$0	$75K	$525K	$2,250K	$7,275K
9-Small Deli ($50K)		$50K	$0	$50K	$500K	$1,500K	$5,800K
10-Sporting Goods ($75K) R		$75K	$0	$75K	$600K	$2,250K	$7,575K
11-Restaurant ($200K), G		$200K	$0	$200K	$1,400K	$6,000K	$19,800K
12-Laundermat ($75K) R		$75K	$0	$75K	$600K	$2,250K	$8,550K
13-Optical Goods ($75K) Pu		$75K	$0	$75K	$450K	$2,250K	$7,275K
14-Auto Parts ($100K) Pu		$100K	$0	$100K	$1,000K	$3,000K	$11,500K
15-Dry Cleaners ($75K) G		$75K	$0	$75K	$600K	$2,250K	$7,575K
16-Mail Box Service ($35K)		$35K	$0	$35K	$350K	$1,050K	$3,955K
17-Jewelry ($100K) Br		$100K	$0	$100K	$500K	$3,000K	$8,600K
18-Home Electronics ($75K) S		$75K	$0	$75K	$750K	$2,250K	$8,400K
19-Meat/Fish/Poultry ($75K)		$75K	$0	$75K	$750K	$2,250K	$8,400K

20-Hardware ($50K)	$50K	$0	$50K	$250K	$1,000K	$3,350K
21-Fruits/Vegetables ($50K)	$50K	$0	$50K	$300K	$1,250K	$4,300K
22-Other Retail ($50K) R	$50K	$0	$50K	$750K	$1,500K	$7,450K
23-Professional's Offices ($150K) Br	$150K	$0	$300K	$1,500K	$4,500K	$17,400K
24-Total Retail		$0	$3,215K	$22,650K	$73,500K	$264,805K
25-Total Business Investment Used		$0	$4,865K	$27,700K	$80,775K	$304,530K
26-Net Monthly Balance		$154K	-$504K	-$437K	$4,403K	$5,706K
27-Cum Balance		$154K	$325K	$726K	$5,706K	

Explanation of Schedule 4

Schedule 4 is the cost of starting the businesses in Schedule 3. Next to each business category is The Company's estimate of how much it will cost to start each business. For example, The Company estimates it will cost $75,00 to open a Small Grocery Store. Since The Company expects to finance 10 Small Grocery Stores in the 4th month the total cost is $750,000 ($75,000 per store times 10 (Schedule 3).

===

NOTES

Schedule 5 – 5 Year Projection of Distributor/ Wholesale & Import Businesses financed by The Company

Schedule 5
Businesses Financed

Distributors/Wholesalers/ Importers	Year 1	Year 2	Year 3	Year 4	Year 5	5 Year Totals
1-Furniture ($200K each) S	15	30	40	80	160	325
2-Home Appliances ($250K) R	15	30	40	75	150	310
3-Women/Girls Clothing ($150K) Y	15	30	40	75	150	310
4-Men/Boys Clothing ($150K) Y	16	35	45	90	180	366
5-Hardware ($100K)	16	35	45	90	180	366
6-Electronics ($150K) Br	16	40	50	50	100	256
7-Auto Products $200K) Bl	16	40	50	50	100	256
8-Food except meat ($250K) Gr	17	40	50	50	100	257
9-Meat/Fish/Poultry ($200K) Gr	17	40	50	100	200	407
10-Beer & Ale ($100K) Pu	16	35	40	80	160	331
11-Restaurant Equipment ($250K), R	17	35	40	80	160	332
12-Distilled Spirits & Wine ($150K) R	16	35	40	80	160	331
13-Jewelry (($100K)	16	35	40	80	160	331
14-Sporting Goods ($100K) Gr	15	35	40	80	160	330
15-Shoes ($75K)	15	35	40	80	160	330
16-Miscellaneous Projects ($100K) BL, Pu, P	15	35	200	400	800	1,450
17- Total Dist./Wholes/Importers	253	506	1,012	2,024	4,048	7,843

Explanation of Schedule 5

The 1st Year of Schedule 5 is equal to the Year 1 Totals from Schedule 1, line 17. The number of businesses financed by The Company is assumed to double every category every year as investment increases.

The Players at the end of 5 Years

The Janitor (silver) has contracts cleaning 25 Furniture Distributors, line 1. His staff is up to 100. In addition he has contracts in retail, government, and industrial establishments.

The Small Construction Company (red) has built 30 Home Appliance Stores (line 2), 35 Restaurants (line 11), and 15 Distilled Spirits & Wine Distributors.

The non-Black Architect (brown) has designed dozens of projects for The Company. He is especially adept at designing Electronics Stores, line 6.

The Married Couple (Yellow) expand their import business as The Company finances more and more businesses. They are supplying 250 businesses at the end of the 5 years, lines 3 and 4.

The Computer Expert (Blue) has secured many contracts to automate some of the businesses that The Company has financed. His contracts include 20 Auto Parts Companies, line 7. He has hired 75 computer whizzes in order to keep up with the demand. The Computer Expert has also started a computer training school that has 10 locations. (See Miscellaneous Projects, line 16).

The Lawyer's (Green) practice has grown so much that he now has 50 lawyers at 10 locations in his firm. See lines 8, 9, and 14.

The Truck Driver (Aqua) has a fleet of 75 trucks delivering goods along the east coast, line 16.

The Grandmother's grandchildren (Pink) are being educated to be future leaders. The eldest one is concentrating on mathematics because she wants to be an architect. There is not enough Black architects for the tasks ahead. The youngest child is a boy interested in flying. We will after all, need our own airlines, line 16.

===

Schedule 6 – The Cost of The Businesses Financed in Schedule 5

Schedule 6	Total Year 1	Year 2	Year 3	Year 4	Year 5	5 Year Totals
Direct Business Loans	$310,236K	$620,472K	$1,240,945K	$2,481,890K	$4,963,781K	$9,617,325K
Distributors/ Wholesalers /Importers						
1-Furniture ($200K each) S	$3,000K	$6,000K	$8,000K	$16,000K	$32,000K	$65,000K
2-Home Appliances ($250K) R	$3,750K	$7,500K	$10,000K	$18,750K	$37,500K	$77,500K
3-Women/Girls Clothing ($150K) Y	$2,250K	$4,500K	$6,000K	$11,250K	$22,500K	$46,500K
4-Men/Boys Clothing ($150K) Y	$2,400K	$5,250K	$6,750K	$13,500K	$27,000K	$54,900K
5-Hardware ($100K)	$1,600K	$3,500K	$4,500K	$9,000K	$18,000K	$36,600K
6-Electronics ($150K) Br	$2,400K	$8,000K	$10,000K	$10,000K	$20,000K	$50,400K
7-Auto Products $200K) Bl	$3,200K	$8,000K	$10,000K	$10,000K	$20,000K	$51,200K
8-Food except meat ($250K) Gr	$4,250K	$10,000K	$12,500K	$12,500K	$25,000K	$64,250K
9-Meat/Fish/Poultry ($200K) Gr	$3,400K	$8,000K	$10,000K	$20,000K	$40,000K	$81,400K
10-Beer & Ale ($100K) Pu	$1,600K	$3,500K	$4,000K	$8,000K	$16,000K	$33,100K
11-Restaurant Equipment ($250K) R	$4,250K	$7,000K	$8,000K	$16,000K	$32,000K	$67,250K
12-Distilled Spirits & Wine ($150K) R	$2,400K	$5,250K	$6,000K	$12,000K	$24,000K	$49,650K

13-Jewelry ((\$100K)	\$1,600K	\$3,500K	\$4,000K	\$8,000K	\$16,000K	\$33,100K
14-Sporting Goods (\$100K) Gr	\$1,500K	\$7,000K	\$8,000K	\$16,000K	\$32,000K	\$64,500K
15-Shoes (\$75K)	\$1,125K	\$2,625K	\$3,000K	\$6,000K	\$12,000K	\$24,750K
16-Miscellaneous Projects (\$100K) Bl,Pu, P	\$1,000K	\$3,500K	\$20,000K	\$40,000K	\$80,000K	\$144,500K
17- Total Dist./ Wholes /Importers	\$39,725K	\$93,125K	\$130,750K	\$227,000K	\$454,000K	\$944,600K

Explanation of Schedule 6

Schedule 6 is the unit cost of each category of business times the number of businesses financed. For example: Furniture Distributors are \$200,000 each. Since there are 15 on Schedule 5 in Year 1(line 1), the total cost to finance them is 15 times \$200,000 = \$3,000,000. The Direct Business Loans is from Exhibit C, line 11, Year 1 Total.

==

NOTES

Schedule 7

Schedule 7	Year 1	Year 2	Year 3	Year 4	Year 5	5 Year Totals
Retail Businesses Financed						
1-Small Grocery Stores ($75K each) Bl	350	500	2,000	2,500	5,000	10,350
2-Medium Grocery Stores ($150K) R	212	300	750	1,500	3,000	5,762
3-Large Grocery Stores ($500K) S	99	200	500	1,000	2,000	3,799
4-Women's Clothing ($75K), O	102	200	500	1,000	2,000	3,802
5-Men's Clothing ($75K) O	102	200	500	1,000	2,000	3,802
6-Shoes ($35K) O	98	150	500	1,000	2,000	3,748
7-Travel Agencies ($20K)	66	100	150	300	600	1,216
8-Furniture ($75K) Pu	97	200	500	1,000	2,000	3,797
9-Small Deli ($50K)	116	200	300	600	1,200	2,416
10-Sporting Goods ($75K) R	101	200	750	1,500	3,000	5,551
11-Restaurant ($200K), G	99	200	300	600	1,200	2,399
12-Laundermat ($75K) R	114	200	300	600	1,200	2,414
13-Optical Goods ($75K) Pu	97	175	25	50	100	447
14-Auto Parts ($100K) Pu	115	225	400	800	1,600	3,140
15-Dry Cleaners ($75K) G	101	200	300	600	1,200	2,401
16-Mail Box Service ($35K)	113	200	300	600	1,200	2,413
17-Jewelry ($100K) Br	84	200	300	600	1,200	2,384
18-Home Electronics ($75K) S	112	200	300	600	1,200	2,412
19-Meat/Fish/Poultry ($75K)	112	200	300	600	1,200	2,412
20-Hardware ($50K)	67	150	250	500	1,000	1,967
21-Fruits/Vegetables ($50K)	86	175	250	500	1,000	2,011
22-Other Retail ($50K) R	149	300	400	800	1,600	3,249
23-Professional's Offices ($150K) Br	116	500	750	2,500	5,000	8,866
24-Total Retail Businesses	2,708	5,175	10,625	20,750	41,500	80,758

25-Total New Businesses	2,961	5,681	11,637	22,774	45,548	88,601

Explanation of Schedule 7

Schedule 7 is the projected number of retail businesses The Company hopes to establish over 5 years.

The Total New Businesses in Year 1 is from Schedule 3, line 25, Year 1 Total.

The Players

Line 1- The Computer Expert has business accounts with over 300 small grocery stores. He also has 25 computer schools on the East Coast.

Lines 2, 10, 12 and 22 – The Small Construction is no longer small. It has built over 350 projects financed by The Company

Lines 3 and 18 – The Janitor has over 500 employees. He has contracts with 200 Company financed businesses alone.

Lines 4, 5 and 6. The Welfare Mother is a fashion mogul. She has design studios in Cape Town, South Africa, Atlanta and Rio. She has 100 stores in the USA, 25 in Asia, 35 in Europe and 20 in Africa.

Line 8, 13 and 14. The Truck Driver has over 100 trucks delivering goods to all manner of businesses.

Line 11 – The Street Corner Brother has 50 first class soul food restaurants all over America. He's thinking about franchising here in Asia and also in Europe.

Line 15 – The Lawyer's law firm is in 20 cities and he's constantly on the lookout for new law school grads.

Lines 17 and 23 – The Non-Black Architect has many clients and become integrated in the Black economic revolution

==

NOTES

Schedule 8 – The Cost of the Retail Businesses Financed in Schedule 7 over 5 Years

Schedule 8

Retail Outlets	Year 1	Year 2	Year 3	Year 4	Year 5	5 Year Totals
1-Small Grocery Stores ($75K each) Bl	$26,250K	$37,500K	$150,000K	$187,500K	$375,000K	$776,250K
2-Medium Grocery Stores ($150K) R	$31,800K	$45,000K	$112,500K	$225,000K	$450,000K	$864,300K
3-Large Grocery Stores ($500K) S	$49,500K	$100,000K	$250,000K	$500,000K	$1,000,000K	$1,899,500K
4-Women's Clothing ($75K), O	$7,650K	$15,000K	$37,500K	$75,000K	$150,000K	$285,150K
5-Men's Clothing ($75K) O	$7,650K	$15,000K	$37,500K	$75,000K	$150,000K	$285,150K
6-Shoes ($35K) O	$3,430K	$5,250K	$17,500K	$35,000K	$70,000K	$131,180K
7-Travel Agencies ($20K)	$1,320K	$2,000K	$3,000K	$6,000K	$12,000K	$24,320K
8-Furniture ($75K) Pu	$7,275K	$15,000K	$37,500K	$75,000K	$150,000K	$284,775K
9-Small Deli ($50K)	$5,800K	$10,000K	$15,000K	$30,000K	$60,000K	$120,800K
10-Sporting Goods ($75K) R	$7,575K	$15,000K	$56,250K	$112,500K	$225,000K	$416,325K
11-Restaurant ($200K), G	$19,800K	$40,000K	$60,000K	$120,000K	$240,000K	$479,800K
12-Laundermat ($75K) R	$8,550K	$15,000K	$22,500K	$45,000K	$90,000K	$181,050K
13-Optical Goods ($75K) Pu	$7,275K	$13,125K	$1,875K	$3,750K	$7,500K	$33,525K
14-Auto Parts ($100K) Pu	$11,500K	$22,500K	$40,000K	$80,000K	$160,000K	$314,000K

15-Dry Cleaners ($75K) G	$7,575K	$15,000K	$22,500K	$45,000K	$90,000K	$180,075K
16-Mail Box Service ($35K)	$3,955K	$7,000K	$10,500K	$21,000K	$42,000K	$84,455K
17-Jewelry ($100K) Br	$8,600K	$20,000K	$30,000K	$60,000K	$120,000K	$238,600K
18-Home Electronics ($75K) S	$8,400K	$15,000K	$22,500K	$45,000K	$90,000K	$180,900K
19-Meat/Fish/ Poultry ($75K)	$8,400K	$15,000K	$22,500K	$45,000K	$90,000K	$180,900K
20-Hardware ($50K)	$3,350K	$7,500K	$12,500K	$25,000K	$50,000K	$98,350K
21-Fruits/ Vegetables ($50K)	$4,300K	$8,750K	$12,500K	$25,000K	$50,000K	$100,550K
22-Other Retail ($50K) R	$7,450K	$15,000K	$20,000K	$40,000K	$80,000K	$162,450K
23-Professional's Offices ($150K) Br	$17,400K	$75,000K	$112,500K	$375,000K	$750,000K	$1,329,900K
24-Total Retail	$264,805K	$528,625K	$1,106,625K	$2,250,750K	$4,501,500K	$8,652,305K
25-Total Business Investment Used	$304,530K	$621,750K	$1,237,375K	$2,477,750K	$4,955,500K	$9,596,905K
26-Net Annual Balance	$5,706K	-$1,277K	$3,570K	$4,140K	$8,281,086	$20,420K
27-Cum Balance	$5,706K	$4,428K	$7,999K	$12,139K	$20,420K	

Explanation of Schedule 8

Schedule 8 is the cost of all retail businesses over 5 years. For example: Small Grocery Stores, Schedule 7, line 1 are $75,000 each to open. There are 350 of them financed in the 1st year on Schedule 7. Therefore the total for the 1st Year for Small Grocery Stores is $26,250,000 ($75,000 times 350). Line 25, Total Business Investment Used = Schedule 6, line 17 (Total Dist/Wholesalers/Importers) + Schedule 8, line 24 (Total Retail Business Costs). Line 26, Net Annual Balance = Exhibit C, line 11 (Direct Loans, Year 1 Total) minus Schedule 8, line 25, Total Business Investment Used. Line 27, Cumulative Balance = The

Annual Cum. Balance + the next years Net Annual Balance. For example Year 1's Cum Balance is $5,706,318.

Year 2's Cum Balance is $4,428,954. That's equal to Year 1's Annual Balance ($5,706,318) plus Year 2's Annual Balance
($-1,277,364).

==

NOTES

Schedule 9

Master Table — Uses of Investment

Business Class	Loan Amount	Number of Loans	Total of Loans$	Loans in Africa	Loans in the USA	Loans in the Carib.	Other	Total New Businesses
Class 1	$200	250K	$50,000K	250K	0	0	0	1,750K
Class 2	$500	200K	$100,000K	200K	0	0	0	1,400K
Class 3	$1,000	150K	$150,000K	125K	10K	5K	10K	1,050K
Class 4	$5,000	125K	$625,000K	50K	40K	5K	30K	875K
Class 5	$7,500	100K	$750,000K	35K	40K	5K	20K	700K
Class 6	$10,000	75K	$750,000K	15K	40K	5K	15K	525K
Class 7	$15,000	60K	$900,000K	15K	30K	3K	12K	420K
Class 8	$20,000	150K	$3,000,000K	30K	100K	5K	15	1,050K
Class 9	$25,000	150K	$3,750,000K	25K	100K	7.5K	17.5K	1,050K
Class 10	$50,000	125K	$6,250,000K	10K	100K	5K	10K	875K
Class 11	$75,000	125K	$9,375,000K	10K	100K	5K	10K	875K
Class 12	$100,000	200K	$20,000,000K	10K	170K	5K	15K	1,400K
Class 14	$250,000	200K	$50,000,000K	10K	170K	5K	15K	1,400K
Class 15 Pu	$500,000	150K	$75,000,000K	10K	120K	5K	15K	1,050K
Class 16 G	$750,000	100K	$75,000,000K	10K	80K	5K	5K	700K
Class 17 Bl	$1,000,000	75K	$75,000,000K	10K	55K	1K	9K	525K
Class 18 O	$2,500,000	20K	$50,000,000K	2K	15.5K	1K	1.5K	140K
Class 19 Y	$5,000,000	20K	$100,000,000K	1.5K	16K	.75K	1.75K	140K
Class 20 Br	$10,000,000	3K	$30,000,000K	.5K	2.15K	.1K	.25K	21K
Class 21 R	$25,000,000	1K	$25,000,000K	.1K	.75K	25	75	7K
Media Bl	$30,000,000	50	$1,500,000K	5	40	2	2	350
Publishing Gr	$5,000,000	20	$100,000K	3	13	1	1	140
Hotels & Resorts, R	$50,000,000	300	$15,000,000K	25	225	20	15	2,100
Transportation Gr	$500,000	200	$100,000K	25	150	10	10	1,400
Real Estate R	$25,000,000	1,160	$29,000,000K	200	850	50	30	8,120
Manufacturing Bl	$25,000,000	1,000	$25,000,000K	250	650	50	20	7,000
Airlines Gr	$75,000,000	15	$1,125,000K	2	11	1	1	105
Misc. Projects P	$100,000	20,000	$2,000,000K	2K	15K	1K	1K	140K
Reserves			$475,000K					
Total New Financed Businesses		2,301,K	$600,000,000K	821K	1,206K	69K	139K	16,112K

Explanation of Schedule 9

This is what The Company believes we can accomplish if we just stick together, respect ourselves and exert willpower. Assume that the 35,000,000 African Americans in The United States of America have a Gross Income of $600,000,000,000.00. What could be done if we invest 10% ($60,000,000,000.00) of that amount annually over 10 years?

The Total Investment over 10 years would be $600,000,000,000.00. This is what Schedule 9 is about.

Schedule 9 divides businesses into Classes based upon how much they cost to finance.

The Class 1 ($200) and Class 2 ($500) businesses are mostly for poor Africans. These loans may buy a sewing machine and enough cloth to produce a sizable number of garments. These are loans not gifts.

As the business loans become larger the more they are concentrated in the United States. There is investment in Africa, Brazil, etc. because we want a global economic empire.

Most of the large individual loans will be for African American business development. For example; there are 200,000 Class 14 businesses. Each Class 14 business costs $250,000 (Loan Amount). That's a total of $50,000,000,000.00 (Total of Loans) over 10 years for Class 14 businesses. Of those 200,000 Class 14 business loans 170,000 are in the USA (Loans in the USA).

Special Businesses are businesses we have to finance in order to control information flow to our people, be respected when we spend a dollar at a resort, and other needs. Right now racist media companies control what we see and hear.

As you can imagine the Players and many others would prosper

===

NOTES

On the lighter side

A few years ago I worked on a project called the AirTrain in New York. The AirTrain is a new rail system that connects Kennedy Airport to the New York City subway system. At one point I was the only man on the staff that were interviewing potential candidates. Christmas was coming so I decided to give each lady a unique gift. I gave lady a one of a kind poem written especially for them. I was considering writing a book of poetry but I got involved in this book. I've included them here and I hope you like them.

Poems

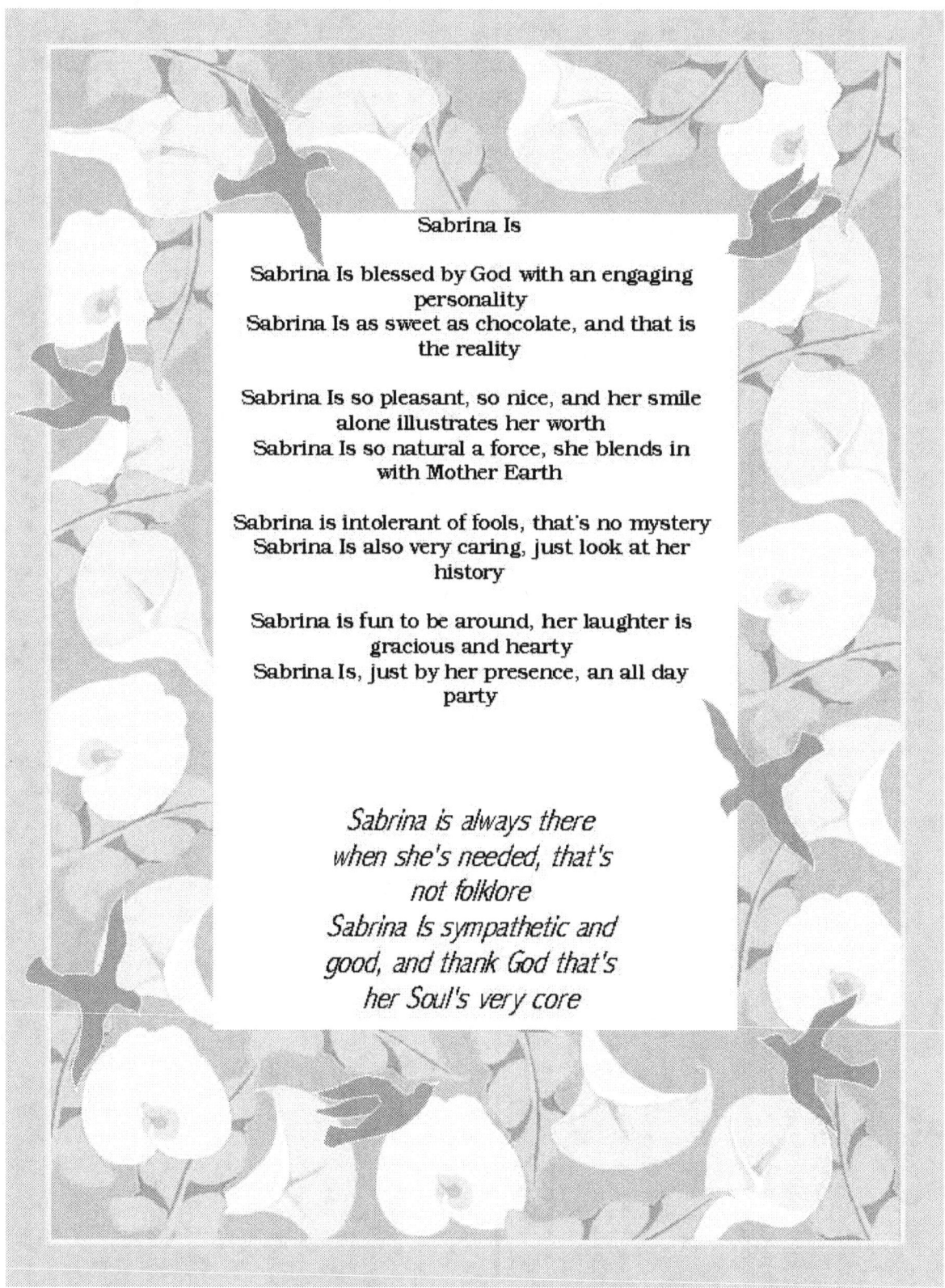

Sabrina Is

Sabrina Is blessed by God with an engaging
personality
Sabrina Is as sweet as chocolate, and that is
the reality

Sabrina Is so pleasant, so nice, and her smile
alone illustrates her worth
Sabrina Is so natural a force, she blends in
with Mother Earth

Sabrina is intolerant of fools, that's no mystery
Sabrina Is also very caring, just look at her
history

Sabrina is fun to be around, her laughter is
gracious and hearty
Sabrina Is, just by her presence, an all day
party

*Sabrina is always there
when she's needed, that's
not folklore
Sabrina Is sympathetic and
good, and thank God that's
her Soul's very core*

Josephine The 1st

Napoleon had his Josephine a long time
ago
Was his Josie as good as ours, I don't think
so

We have our Josephine here in New York,
here and now
We're fortunate beyond belief, and how!

Our Josie is kind of heart and quick of
smile
Our Josie is always a pleasure to be
around, all the while

Josie knows about this and Josie knows
about that
Try to fool her, you'd do better trying to pull
a rabbit out of a hat

Napoleon had his Josephine but she's no
longer on the scene
Here in our presence is the original, the 1st

Gerri Always Knows

Gerri always knows how to enter a room with style and grace
Gerri always knows what will bring a smile to another's face

Gerri always knows how to make the human spirit soar
Gerri always knows that she has class and charisma galore

Gerri always knows how to sooth you when you're blue
Gerri also knows when to be deliciously wise too

Gerri always knows she's unique as can be
Gerri should know she's special, everyone says so, you see

A million years from now when the Angels are bored and can't
find a thing to do
They will even ask Jesus, and he will be out of ideas too

Then Jesus will look around and say, "Lets ask her"
The Archangel Gabriel and St. Peter will agree, because Gerri
always knows

Cheryl, Trinidad Love

She has a very high, light, angelic voice
When you hear it, you must succumb,
you have no choice

Daughter of the grandest Caribbean
Isle, Trinidad, you see
She now graces New York, a diamond of
a gift, from the faraway sea

You are drawn to her you see, like a
moth to a flame
Once you've felt her touch, you will
never be the same

She's strong, she's sly, and like candy
she's sweet
Others can only turn green with envy,
they know they can't complete

She was sent to us by The Almighty
above
Her name is Cheryl, from the house of
Jackson, Trinidad Love

Philippa, Renaissance Light

She's always here, she's always there, and she's always in
demand
If anyone can get the job done, you know Renaissance Light
can

She's cultured, she's modern, and she's knowledgeable to a
fault
If she catches you in a logic trap with your shallow thoughts,
then you have to halt

She's gifted with a superior mind, which she can unleash at
any time
When she uses it, God help you, because it will be too late
to whine

She's the ultimate insider, within the Halls of Power
she's comfortably at ease
When others are blind to the obvious or even the
hidden solutions, she always sees

Light as we all know, travels at an amazingly high
speed
PK's even faster, tell her to slow down, that's advice
you know she will not heed

The Queen knows you better than you even know you
The Queen knows the past, the present and the future too

The Queen is the personification of the Power of the Mind, of
The Body and of The Soul
The Queen does not have to ask anyone about anything, The
Queen already knows

The Queen always looks great, everyone knows that's a fact
The Queen does not have to fake anything, The Queen is a
natural, The Queen does not have to act

The Queen will call your hand if The Queen knows you're wrong
The Queen is also merciful, The Queen always help the weak be
strong

The Queen has no equal and on that everyone is clear
We, The Queen's subjects, are just thankful that The Queen of
Joyce is here

Lillie Frances and Venus

Lillie Frances, according to legend, was from the very start
was a genuine Southern Belle
Venus, The Goddess of Love, resides in the hearts of all
men and there she will always dwell

Lillie Frances, a dark angel, was born with the joy of Life and
a disarming smile
Venus, her friend, is always near, yet far away, can make
men slaves with her guile

Lillie Frances, an ebony beauty can break a heart without
even trying
Venus, can break nations, you know it's true, you know I'm
not lying

Lillie Frances, in your matnificence, would you please have
mercy on men
Venus, you have the wisdom, and the experience, please tell
us mortals how to find love and where to begin

Lillie Frances and Venus have finally been exposed, we know
their game
Admit it, Lillie Frances; we know that you and Venus, The
Goddess of Love, are one in the same

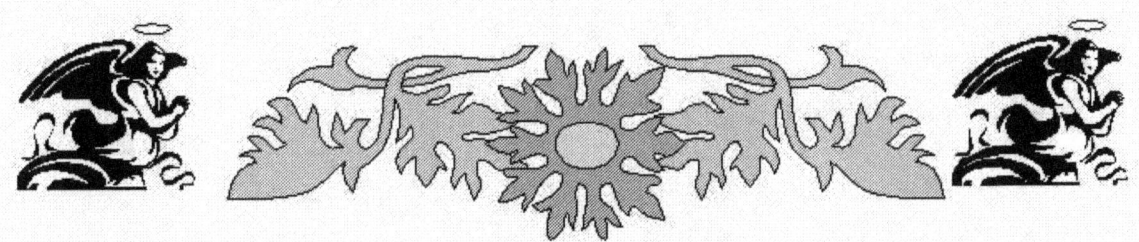

Carolyn The Great

She's like a fresh rainfall in early Spring
She's a presence so elegant your heart will sing

She's cool, she's warm and always sublime
She transcends time and space, she never leaves your mind

She's here, she's there, she's invisible and yet she can be seen
She's night, she's day, she's everthing in between

She's new, she's now, she's the future to be
She's the Sister of the Sun and the Mother of the Sea

She's all that, she's all that and more
She's sleek, she's fast, she's feminine to the core

She's so special, an entity only God could create
No, she's not an illusion, she is of course, Carolyn The Great

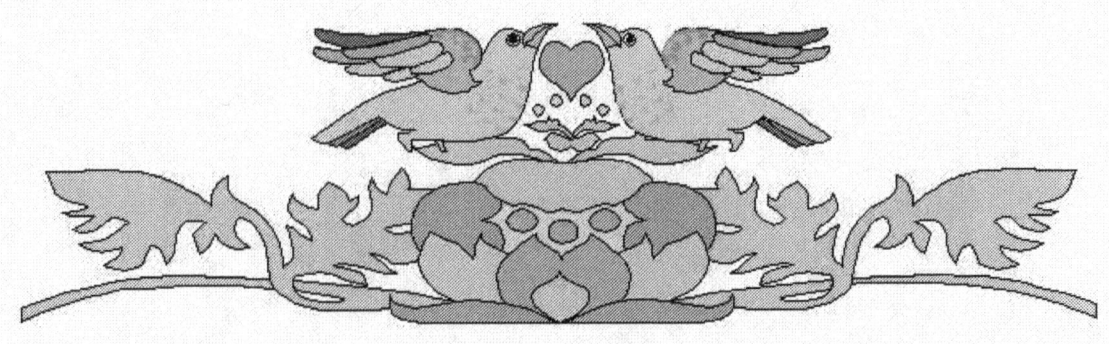

Epilogue

I hope you like the poetry. I just saw the movie Catwoman. Almost every critic said it was terrible but I found it entertaining. After all, it's a comic character. The critics gave it 1 star and said don't waste your money. After seeing Catwoman I can understand why the critics hated it. Halle Berry was just too beautiful. I think the green monster has arisen. They hate the movie because Halle is so beautiful and that beauty and it shows in this movie.

As I said before I was in the United States Air force. The thing that Black airmen are most proud of is the performance of the Tuskegee Airmen. They never lost an American bomber to German fighters. Anybody who knows German flying ability realizes that this is an incredible feat.

This is off the subject but I was just thinking about music. A few times in your life you hear a piece of music that stuns you. The first time it happened I was a boy in South Carolina. The song was Ray Charles' version of a Country and Western song, I Can't Stop Loving you. The radio station played it several times in a row but we couldn't get enough of it. It happened when I used to watch TV with my father. We would watch the Victory At Sea series. The music was exceptional and I still love it today. That's why I recommended it when reading this book.

It happened when I was in the Air Force in California. One Saturday morning an airman friend of mine came to get me out of bed in the barracks. I was hung over and didn't want to get up. He insisted that I come to his room and listen to this new album he had. He played Isaac Hayes' classic album Hot Buttered Soul. I couldn't believe it was possible to accomplish something like this in music. Ike's version of By The Time I Get To Phoenix written by Jim Webb was unworldly. If you want to hear a beautiful love ballad listen to James Brown's Prisoner Of Love.

There you have it. I can't think of anything to add that will make it more doable. Of course there are strategies and concepts that I can't print in this book for obvious reasons. Everything will be legal and in our interests. We have to remind others that although many Black people were born at night, it wasn't last night!

In conclusion, I suggest that we adapt the philosophy of the Bruce Lee, the great martial artist. When it comes to life, we must adjust to the situation, not complain. When water is in a cup it takes the shape of the cup, it always adjusts to its environment. As Mr. Lee said,
"BE WATER, MY FRIEND"

About The Author

Mr. Cliff Bussey has devoted 25 years to finding a solution to Black economic weakness. Mr. Bussey is a United States Air Force Veteran. He graduated from Fordham University in New York City with a degree in Economics and Business.

Mr. Bussey believes he has finally found the solution. This book reprints his vision.